Making Integration Work

Language Training for Adult Migrants

OECD

BETTER POLICIES FOR BETTER LIVES

This work is published under the responsibility of the Secretary-General of the OECD. The opinions expressed and arguments employed herein do not necessarily reflect the official views of OECD member countries.

This document, as well as any data and map included herein, are without prejudice to the status of or sovereignty over any territory, to the delimitation of international frontiers and boundaries and to the name of any territory, city or area.

The statistical data for Israel are supplied by and under the responsibility of the relevant Israeli authorities. The use of such data by the OECD is without prejudice to the status of the Golan Heights, East Jerusalem and Israeli settlements in the West Bank under the terms of international law.

Note by Turkey
The information in this document with reference to "Cyprus" relates to the southern part of the Island. There is no single authority representing both Turkish and Greek Cypriot people on the Island. Turkey recognises the Turkish Republic of Northern Cyprus (TRNC). Until a lasting and equitable solution is found within the context of the United Nations, Turkey shall preserve its position concerning the "Cyprus issue".

Note by all the European Union Member States of the OECD and the European Union
The Republic of Cyprus is recognised by all members of the United Nations with the exception of Turkey. The information in this document relates to the area under the effective control of the Government of the Republic of Cyprus.

Please cite this publication as:
OECD (2021), *Language Training for Adult Migrants*, Making Integration Work, OECD Publishing, Paris, *https://doi.org/10.1787/02199d7f-en*.

ISBN 978-92-64-40345-1 (print)
ISBN 978-92-64-33349-9 (pdf)

Making Integration Work
ISSN 2522-7718 (print)
ISSN 2522-7726 (online)

Foreword

This is the fifth publication in "Making Integration Work", a series that summarises the main lessons from the OECD's work on integration policies. The objective is to summarise in a non-technical way the main challenges and good policy practices to support the lasting integration of immigrants and their children in the host countries.

This fifth edition takes stock of the experiences of OECD countries with respect to language training for adult migrants, exploring a number of policy lessons with supporting examples of good practice. It also provides a comprehensive comparison of the policy frameworks that govern integration policy for adult migrants in OECD countries. Information about the different policy frameworks was gathered through a questionnaire sent to member countries.

Previous editions of this series addressed the integration of refugees and others in need of protection, the assessment and recognition of foreign qualifications, integration of family migrants, and integration of young people with migrant parents.

Acknowledgements

This booklet was written by Lauren Matherne and Anne-Sophie Senner, under the co-ordination of Thomas Liebig from the OECD's International Migration Division. It includes contributions from Cécile Thoreau, Emily Farchy, and Thomas Huddleston (consultant to the OECD). It benefitted from comments from Jean-Christophe Dumont (OECD). The OECD developed this publication with financial support from the German Federal Ministry of the Interior, Building and Community. It also benefitted from seed money for the series "Making Integration Work" through grants from the German Federal Ministry for Family Affairs, Senior Citizens, Women and Youth, the Norwegian Ministry of Education and Research, the Swedish Ministry of Employment and the King Baudouin Foundation (Belgium). This work would not have been possible without the support of the members of the OECD's Working Party on Migration and the national authorities in charge of asylum and integration policy, who willingly shared their knowledge of national policy frameworks and programmes.

Table of contents

FIGURES

TABLES

Follow OECD Publications on:

http://twitter.com/OECD_Pubs

http://www.facebook.com/OECDPublications

http://www.linkedin.com/groups/OECD-Publications-4645871

http://www.youtube.com/oecdilibrary

OECD Alerts http://www.oecd.org/oecddirect/

Introduction

Why is language training for adult migrants an important issue?

Working knowledge of a host country's language is the tool that allows migrants to participate fully in host-country society. Without competent levels of language learning, other important masteries will elude migrants; thus, language is arguably the most important host-country related skill for migrants to develop. Speaking the host-country language allows migrants to access services and communicate their needs effectively. To succeed on local labour markets, migrants must be able to communicate with employers, hiring managers, and colleagues. Language also plays an important role in the creation of community and a sense of belonging. Immigrants who speak the host-country language have greater social contacts with native speakers and are more likely to pursue higher education opportunities than immigrants with little or no command of the host-country language.[1] While there is little comparative information available on language mastery of immigrants across the OECD, 2014 data for European OECD countries and Australia show that two-thirds of foreign-born in the EU state they have at least advanced proficiency in a host-country language. In Australia, where two in five migrants have English as their mother tongue, the share is even higher, at 70%. However, the shares vary from about 20% in Estonia to about 90% in Hungary, Luxembourg, and Portugal (Figure 1).

Figure 1. Advanced host-country language proficiency (percentages of foreign-born 15-64 year-olds, 2014), European OECD countries and Australia

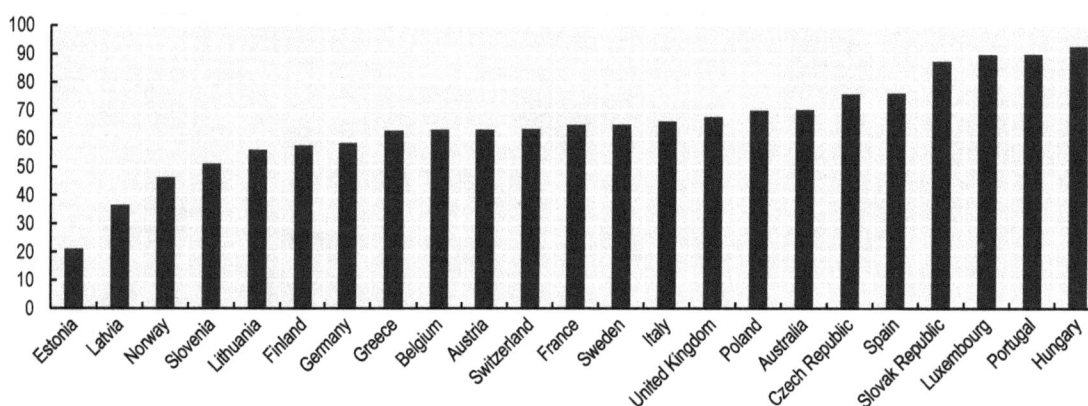

Source: OECD and EU (2018), Settling In 2018, https://doi.org/10.1787/9789264307216-en

In all countries, longer residence is associated with better knowledge of the host-country language. Across the EU, among recently arrived non-native speakers, attending a language course in the host country has been associated with an 8 percentage point greater likelihood of proficiency in the host language (OECD/EU, 2018). Not surprisingly then, language training is the principal component of introduction programmes for new arrivals and represents the bulk of government expenditures on immigrant integration in almost all OECD countries. Putting in place effective language training for adult migrants should provide a high return on investment, particularly in countries with a high share of humanitarian migrants,[2] who often have little-to-no proficiency in the host-country language. To be effective, however, training must be designed to match individual needs. Across the OECD, countries have become increasingly aware of the need to better integrate working-age migrants and seek to improve the capacity and performance of their language training schemes.

Speaking the host-country language is the single most important determinant for labour market integration

Although difficult to measure, it is generally conceived that mastery of the host-country language is the single most important characteristic that allows an individual immigrant to participate and succeed in the host-country labour market (OECD, 2018). Immigrants who speak the host-country language have significantly higher employment rates than those who report language difficulties – independent of the reason for migration and the level and origin of qualifications (Zorlu and Hartog, 2018). How well immigrants master the host-country language also determines whether and to what extent they can use their qualifications. After controlling for differences in other observable characteristics, immigrants in employment who have difficulties in the host-country language have over-qualification rates that are 17 percentage points higher than similar immigrants who speak the host-country language well (Damas de Matos and Liebig, 2014). Moreover, gaps in unemployment and employment rates between foreign and native-born populations remain significant in most OECD countries, with some notable exceptions. Host countries have thus enacted a variety of measures to reduce barriers to labour-market insertion, with an increasing focus on language education.

To be effective, language training must be oriented towards labour market integration and reflect the unique challenges of adult language-learning

Despite the importance of language proficiency for labour market integration, language training has often only limited association with labour market performance (Liebig and Huddleston, 2014). In part, this reflects the challenge of designing language programmes targeted to adults. For decades, research on language learning examined age in the context of "sensitive" or "critical" periods for learning, often concluding that adults could only rarely reach near-native proficiency. However, it has been more recently acknowledged that there is substantial variability among mature learners, and that there may be ways to better support adult language learning that employ a variety of learning techniques and acknowledge the impact of external factors (Kozar and Yates, 2019). Second-language learning is a complex process, especially for adults experiencing concurrent integration challenges. Adults not only are more instrumentally motivated than children, but also must balance competing demands on their time, specifically providing for themselves financially, and can be demotivated when the immediate benefit of learning is not apparent. Indeed, participating in language training might prevent immigrants from actively seeking or gathering work experience, which, in turn, sends negative signals to employers who tend to avoid job applicants with long absences from the labour market (Clausen et al., 2009). The additional months of non-employment are costly both for the migrant and the host country. One way to avoid such "lock-in" effects is to adjust the content and objectives of language training to labour market needs. Flexibility in the schedule and duration of language courses can also encourage more effective participation by adult migrants. Vocation-specific language training, ideally provided on the job, has proven highly effective in this regard (Friedenberg, 2014). However, to date, relatively few courses of this format exist in OECD countries, as such training tends to be costly and difficult to organise.

The purpose of this booklet

Designing effective language training is a challenging task. Whether or not immigrants make progress and can apply these skills to the labour market depends not only on how well language training is geared towards labour market integration. It also relies on the quality of available language learning options and on how well these are targeted to individual abilities and needs. Finally, success reflects immigrants' motivation to learn and depends on the accessibility and affordability of available language learning options. This policy-oriented booklet guides policy makers and practitioners through the design and implementation of effective language programmes for adult migrants. The term adult migrant is used throughout this volume to describe foreign-born migrants, regardless of their motivation for migration, who arrived in their host country at an age that renders them ineligible for mainstream education, including language training (typically from the age of 18). Where countries have implemented programmes that apply solely to specific groups of migrants – such as humanitarian migrants or labour migrants – they have been so identified.

Drawing on experience from OECD countries[3] and a number of empirical studies, this booklet presents 12 lessons and examples of good practice, which policy makers can use to increase the benefits of language training for immigrants, employers, and society at large. Several lessons focus on ensuring migrant participation in language courses, for example by **ensuring access, even for settled migrants**. Defining eligibility to participate in language programmes as broadly as possible will allow governments to reach a greater number of migrants. The timing of access is also important. New arrivals should have **access to language training as early as possible** so that they can effectively navigate their life in the host country. To motivate migrant participation, countries should **design incentives rather than relying mainly on sanctions**. Whereas incentive-based policies can enhance migrants' intrinsic motivation to learn, sanctions may have unintended negative effects. Affordability is also a consideration, **as cost should not be an obstacle to language learning**. Countries have taken a variety of approaches to this challenge, from providing language courses free of charge to using a deposit model in which migrants receive reimbursement upon successful completion of a course. Lastly, **language training should be flexible and compatible with other life constraints**. Adult migrants must fit language training into their day alongside job and child-care obligations. Policy decisions such as provision of childcare during classes can make this easier.

Later lessons are designed to help policy-makers improve the language courses themselves by developing programmes that meet the needs of the migrant population. Many language courses are not particularly relevant or sufficient for the realities of the labour market and thus do not meet the needs of a large number of migrants. To address this, language courses should be **integrated with vocational training or designed in co-operation with employers** where feasible. Before placing migrants in a course, it is important to **assess each learner's level of education and capacity to learn**. This will ensure to the greatest extent possible that migrants are placed in a course where they can be successful. **Engagement with language specialists and non-traditional partners** will broaden learning opportunities. Involvement of stakeholders outside the policy-making sphere, such as educators and private-sector partners, improves quality and agility in developing new programming. Especially where several stakeholders – within and across levels of government – play a role, it is important to **ensure co-ordination between all relevant stakeholders and defining common standards**. A central actor in charge of co-ordination can ensure that standards are met efficiently and consistently. Governments can also **encourage development of new technologies**. While questions of equality of access must be considered, it is clear there is untapped potential in the trend toward digitalisation, particularly in how it allows governments to expand their course offerings and increase flexibility. To capitalise on these innovations, governments need to **invest in teacher preparation and recruitment**. Teacher shortages remain a barrier to ensuring all migrants have access to the language courses they need. To attract and retain more and better teachers, it is important to provide these professionals with the preparation and support they require to succeed in their roles, particularly in an increasingly high-tech environment.

Finally, both for questions of access and course quality, it is vital **to evaluate the impact of language training on migrant integration**. Given the substantial investment in language programmes for adult migrants in many countries, there is significant interest in knowing which practices achieve the best results. The final lesson of this booklet notes however that language programmes are rarely formally evaluated and provides considerations for conducting thorough, informative assessments of these programmes.

1. Ensure access to language training, including for settled migrants

WHAT and WHY?

Having access to publicly organised and subsidised language training is for many migrants a critical condition for learning the language of their new country of residence. Where immigrants, and new arrivals in particular, are ineligible to participate in public language programmes, they may find it difficult to identify adequate and affordable learning options in their area, which in turn may delay their integration. Moreover, denying certain groups the right to participate in publicly arranged and subsidised language programmes may signal to those migrants that their integration into the host country is not desired. Recognising this, many publicly funded language programmes in OECD countries are gradually opening to a growing number of new arrivals, including asylum seekers and intra-EU migrants in some cases.

WHO?

Public language training programmes should be open to all immigrants in need who are expected to remain in the country. This includes long-term residents with limited proficiency in the host-country language – independent of whether or not they are looking for a job and are eligible to receive benefits. Reunited family members and resettled refugees are important target groups in this regard. New arrivals, who may initially come on a temporary permit, should also have access. In addition, an increasing number of countries, such as Germany and the United Kingdom, have opened language programmes to nationals and made them obligatory for unemployed working-age adults with limited language skills.

HOW?

Establishing a right to participate in language training for all immigrant adults in need who are expected to remain in the country is a crucial first step to encourage successful economic and social integration. To date, most OECD countries grant legal access to public language training programmes to all legally resident foreigners (see Table 1.1). Portugal makes language training available to all migrants with a pending residency or asylum application, and in the United States, many language programmes are available to adults regardless of visa status. Most programmes in Western European countries, with some exceptions such as France, Norway, and Spain, are now open to both EU and non-EU citizens. However, a lack of information or awareness about available learning options sometimes prevents potential learners from participating (see Lesson 2). Mainstreaming the supply of language courses and fully integrating them into other training programmes, such as Active Labour Market Policies (ALMPs), is a way to make sure that language training is proposed to all eligible immigrant adults, facilitating their participation. Australia, Belgium, Czech Republic, Germany, Denmark, Finland, France, the Netherlands and Norway are among the OECD countries that have established dedicated policies aimed at including language training in mainstream services to immigrants, albeit to varying degrees.

Additionally, a long eligibility period (see Table 1.2) will help governments reach a greater number of migrants. Such prolonged periods are designed to recognise that those who access work earlier may be less likely to put aside time for language learning, but that it may still be important for their professional advancement and long-term integration.

Table 1.1. Eligibility to publicly (co-) financed language training for migrants in OECD countries, 2020 or latest available year

	Migrants with refugee status and beneficiaries of subsidiary protection	Migrants benefitting from other forms of protection	Newly arrived adult family migrants	Newly arrived labour migrants	Longer-term residents	EU countries only: Newly arrived EU citizens
Australia	Yes	Yes (if they hold an eligible visa)	Yes (if they hold an eligible visa)	Yes	Yes (if they hold an eligible visa and register within 6 months of receiving this visa)	/
Austria	Yes	No	Yes (if labour market access is granted)	No	Yes (via PES if registered as un-employed, but no legal entitlement)	Yes (via PES if registered as un-employed, but no legal entitlement)
Belgium	Yes	Yes	Yes	Yes	Yes	Yes
Canada	Yes	Yes (if they maintain permanent resident status)	Yes	Yes	Yes (until acquisition of citizenship)	/
Chile	No	No	No	No	No	/
Colombia	/	/	/	/	/	/
Czech Republic	Yes	Yes	Yes	Yes	Yes	No
Denmark	Yes	Yes	Yes	Yes	Yes	Yes
Estonia	Yes	/	Yes	Yes	Yes	Yes
Finland	Yes	Yes	Yes	No (except ESF-funded on-the-job, language training for migrant workers or in the case of state- or municipally-funded programmes)	No (although unemployment benefits are available for those who study Finnish or Swedish)	Yes
France	Yes	/	Yes	Yes	No	No
Germany	Yes	Yes	Yes	Yes	Yes	Yes
Greece	Yes (not systematic)	Yes	Yes	Yes	Yes	/
Hungary	Not systematic but some funded by ERF and Ministry of Interior)	Yes, for migrants with temp. protection under DIR 2001/55/EC	Yes	Yes	Yes	No
Iceland	/	/	/	/	/	/

	Migrants with refugee status and beneficiaries of subsidiary protection	Migrants benefitting from other forms of protection	Newly arrived adult family migrants	Newly arrived labour migrants	Longer-term residents	EU countries only: Newly arrived EU citizens
Ireland	Yes	Yes	Yes	Yes	Yes	Yes
Israel	No	No	Yes (if they hold new immigrant status)	Yes (if they hold new immigrant status)	No	No
Italy	Yes	Yes	Yes	Yes	Yes	Yes
Japan	Yes (Convention refugees and certain resettled refugees, who are actively engaged in job-search)	No	Yes (family of nationals, perm + long-term residents and refugees in active job-search)	No	Yes (if actively engaged in job-search)	/
Korea	Yes	Yes	Yes	Yes	Yes	/
Latvia	Yes	Yes	Yes	Yes	Yes	Yes
Lithuania	Yes	Yes	Yes	No	No	/
Luxembourg	Yes	Yes	Yes	Yes	Yes	Yes
Mexico	Yes	No	No	No	No	/
Netherlands	Yes (loan-based but those who pass the exam within the established period do not have to pay it back)	Yes (loan-based but those who pass the exam within the established period do not have to pay it back)	Yes (loan-based)	Yes (loan-based)	Yes (loan-based)	Yes (loan-based)
New Zealand	Yes	Yes (if they hold New Zealand residence)	Depends on sponsor (Yes for holders of a residence visa; No for accompanying family of new residents who must cover entire costs)	Yes (if they hold a residence visa)	Yes	/
Norway	Yes	Yes	Yes	No (obliged to pay fee to provider to participate in language training)	Yes	No
Poland	Yes (in the framework of the integration programme)	No	No	No	No	No
Portugal	Yes	Yes	Yes	Yes	Yes	Yes
Slovak Republic	Yes	/	No (but free language courses organised by the IOM in Bratislava and Košice)	No (but free language courses organised by the IOM in Bratislava and Košice)	No (but free language courses organised by the IOM in Bratislava and Košice)	No (but free language courses organised by the IOM in Bratislava and Košice)
Slovenia	Yes	No	Yes	Yes	Yes	No
Spain	Yes	Yes	Yes	Yes	Yes	No
Sweden	Yes	Yes	Yes	Yes	Yes	Yes
Switzerland	Yes	Yes	Yes	Yes	Yes	Yes

	Migrants with refugee status and beneficiaries of subsidiary protection	Migrants benefitting from other forms of protection	Newly arrived adult family migrants	Newly arrived labour migrants	Longer-term residents	EU countries only: Newly arrived EU citizens
Turkey	Yes	Yes	Yes	Yes	Yes	/
United Kingdom	Yes (ESOL and DCLG community programme)	Yes (ESOL and DCLG community programme)	Yes (eligible to DCLG community programme but not a target group; eligible to ESOL training but only after 3 years of residence for family members of labour migrants)	No (but eligible to ESOL training if they have been resident for at least 3 years)	Yes (ESOL and DCLG community programme)	Yes (eligible to ESOL if they have been resident for at least 3 years; eligible to DCLG community programme but not a target group)
United States	Yes	Yes	Yes	Yes	Yes	/

Note: n.a. = information not available. This information is based on a 2017 questionnaire and 2020 updates by member countries.
Source: OECD questionnaire on language training for adult migrants 2017.

Table 1.2. Eligibility to publicly (co-) financed language training for migrants in OECD countries, 2020 or latest available year

	Conditions for eligibility other than the migrant's category	Time limit after which migrants are no longer eligible
Australia	Having less than vocational English	Effective April 2021, migrants arriving after 1 October 2020 must: • register with an AMEP service provider within 6 months (or 12 months if under 18 years of age at the time of registration), • commence tuition within 12 months, • complete tuition within 5 years from the date of visa commencement or arrival in Australia Applications for extensions are possible within a 10-year limit. Migrants in Australia prior to 1 October are not subject to time limitations for commencing or completing AMEP tuition.
Austria	• Having labour market access (adult family migrants) • For PES courses, eligibility is conditional on registration as unemployed (longer-term residents and EU nationals) • No further conditions for refugees	• Yes (adult family migrants: the first module of language training must be completed within 2 years of signing the obligatory integration agreement) • No (people entitled to asylum or subsidiary protection, unemployed longer-term residents and unemployed EU nationals)
Belgium	No	No
Canada i	No (but all eligible Settlement Program clients must be of legal age to leave school within their applicable province/territory)	No (acquisition of citizenship ends eligibility for the Settlement Program; ineligible clients may be eligible for provincially- and territorially-funded services)
Chile	/ (no language training is provided)	/
Colombia	/	/
Czech Republic	No	• No (for adult family migrants, newly arrived labour migrants and long-term residents) • Yes (for humanitarian migrants and their subsidiaries in the framework of the state integration programme: 12 months from reception of residence title)
Denmark	No	• 5 years (refugees, adult family migrants arrived via family reunification)

	Conditions for eligibility other than the migrant's category	Time limit after which migrants are no longer eligible
		• Up to 3.5 years of ordinary Danish courses (labour migrants, international students, adult family migrants arrived as accompanying spouses)
Estonia	No	• 2 years (refugees and beneficiaries of subsidiary protection) • 5 years (newly arrived adult family migrants and EU-citizens in the framework of the Welcoming programme; other publicly financed language trainings have no time limit) • No time limit (longer-term residents)
Finland	Mainly provided to unemployed migrants who are registered	• 3 years after receiving the first residence permit, can be extended to 5 • Finnish citizens are excluded from participation
France	Insufficient French language skills (below level A1)ⁱⁱ	1 year from signing the integration contract (CIR)
Germany	• Holding a legal long-term residence title valid for at least for one year (for all except asylum seekers) • Having a good perspective of staying in Germany (asylum seekers)	No
Greece	No, other than having the necessary legal residence documents	No
Hungary	No	No (except for migrants benefitting from temporary protection: 24 months from status recognition)
Iceland		
Ireland	Priority is given to those in need of Basic English language skills to a level of functional competency	No
Israel	• Holding new immigrant status / being Jewish or first-class family member of a Jewish migrant • Being over 17 years of age (under the age of 17 language training is provided in the public-school system)	18 months within reception of new immigrant status (24 months for immigrants entitled to income support)
Italy	No	30 credits in 2 years under Integration Agreement
Japan	• Being actively engaged in job-search • Type of sponsor for (family migrants)	No (but resettled refugees are expected to complete language training within 6 months of arrival)
Korea	No	No
Latvia	Asylum seekers, refugees, and their subsidiaries have no additional criteria. Being registered as unemployed and/or seeking employment is a criteria for other migrant categories	No
Lithuania	No	15 – 36 months depending on migrants' vulnerability
Luxembourg	• No (refugees, persons with subsidiary protection status, asylum seekers) • Yes (temporary protection, family migrants, labour migrants, longer-term residents, EU nationals: referral by the integration office, labour market agency or social office)	2 years from signing the welcome and integration contract
Mexico	No	No
Netherlands	Having insufficient income/means to pay for a language course	• 5 years upon arrival/reception of residence status for humanitarian migrants • 3 years from receiving a letter of Civic Integration for family migrants
New Zealand	Holding a residence visa (migrants on temporary visas have to pay an additional fee and accompanying family members of new residents must cover the entire costs themselves)	No maximum period except some specialist ESOL programmes: 5 years for intensive literacy and numeracy ESOL; 3 years for fee-free programmes for refugees studying at Level 3+ ESOL; 5 years for accompanying family members of new residents)
Norway	Yes	• 3 years plus documented absence time for participants with less than upper secondary

	Conditions for eligibility other than the migrant's category	Time limit after which migrants are no longer eligible
		education • 18 months plus documented absence time for those with at least upper secondary education
Poland	Receiving social assistance	12 months (for refugees)
Portugal	All legally resident adult immigrants (aged 18 years and older) are eligible. Since August 2020, eligibility has been extended to those who do not yet have legal status, provided a residence permit or asylum application has been submitted and the procedure is pending. A Social Security Identification Number must have been allocated.	No
Slovak Republic	Staying in the asylum centre (for refugees and persons with subsidiary protection)	As long as they reside in asylum centre (for refugees and persons with subsidiary protection status)
Slovenia	No (except from holding a valid residence permit)	• No (asylum seekers, humanitarian migrants, newly arrived adult family migrants and longer-term migrants) • Yes (newly arrived labour migrants: 1 year)
Spain	No	No
Sweden	Lacking basic knowledge of Swedish	No
Switzerland	No (but priority is given to people with social disadvantages and special needs)	No
Turkey	No	No
United Kingdom	• Being benefit-dependant • Minimum of 3 years residency for labour migrants, family members of labour migrants and EU nationals • No for eligibility to DCLG community programme but priority is given to isolated longer-term residents with the lowest levels of English	No
United States	Having another native language than English or living in a family or community where a language other than English is the dominant language	No

Notes: n.a. = information not available; See Table 1.1.

i. Unless otherwise indicated, all references to Canada in this publication refer to programming at the federal level and do not represent programming funded by other levels of government.

ii. The Common European Framework of Reference for Languages (CEFR), is a guideline used to describe achievements of learners of foreign languages across Europe and, increasingly, in other countries. The CEFR categorises language proficiency in six levels, A1 to C2, defined by "can do" descriptors. https://www.coe.int/en/web/common-european-framework-reference languages/level-descriptions.

Source: OECD questionnaire on language training for adult migrants 2017.

2. Make sure that new arrivals get language training early

WHAT and WHY?

The first years after arriving in the host-country are a critical timespan for new arrivals, who need to acquaint themselves with public institutions and available services and understand the functioning of the local labour market. Newcomers have fewer coping mechanisms than migrants who have been present in the host country for longer periods. Early intervention to alleviate language difficulties can prevent lock-in effects that reduce migrant outcomes. Learning the host-country language early also implies that learners are younger, which facilitates the learning process and increases migrants' motivation and the returns on their investment – with important benefits for them and for the host-country.

WHO?

Early language training should be a priority for all new arrivals with limited proficiency in the host-country language. Often, however, the timing of access to language training depends on the channel of migration. While successful asylum claimants may be the group that most needs language training, this group often waits longest to access language programmes, depending on the duration of the asylum procedure. Some countries have tried to counter long periods of inactivity by providing language training to asylum seekers while their application is still pending (see Table 2.1). For reuniting family members and resettled refugees, learning should ideally start prior to arrival, namely once a visa has been secured.

HOW?

Early intervention requires that migrants are informed about and referred to available language learning options as early as possible. This can be done through:

- Pre-arrival language screening or training
- Contact with outreach staff in the migrant's native language
- Increasing the number of available courses and hiring more teachers

Some OECD countries, including the Netherlands, Austria, Germany, Hungary, Italy, and Korea, provide information sessions and language training prior to departure in major origin countries, so that new arrivals already possess basic language skills when entering their new country of residence. Such sessions will be most effective when linked to the curricula of post-arrival language training, thereby guaranteeing continuity in the integration pathway. Pre-departure integration programmes could also significantly improve outcomes in family reunification, as family members arriving without a job face different challenges from their petitioning family member. They will not have the same contact with native speakers in the host country on arrival as a working principal immigrant. Once in the country, migrants who arrive without prior training and those who require further training need to undergo an individual assessment (see Lesson 7), whereupon they should be referred to appropriate language programmes by the competent immigration authority or public employment service.

Reaching migrants with limited knowledge of the host-country language may also require advertisement in foreign-languages in immigrant media and frequently visited areas, as well as face-to-face contacts from outreach staff. More detailed print materials as well as a comprehensive online portal can provide an overview of the full range of available language learning options and of course-providers by area (see Box 2.1).[4]

Box 2.1. Disseminating information on language courses to prospective migrants and new arrivals in Canada and New Zealand

Canada informs prospective migrants and new arrivals about the importance of learning English or French, outlines to them the course enrolment process, and provides them with contact information of the closest language assessment centre and the closest provider of general or employment-related language training via the "Welcome to Canada" resource for settlement-related information. Users can also access an online self-assessment test in English or French (CLB-OSA/NCLC AEL) to estimate their current level of proficiency before doing a formal assessment. In addition, immigrants preparing to move to Canada receive free information and individual advice on language and vocational training options through the free Immigrant Integration Programme (CIIP) in a wide range of countries of origin.

Migrants to New Zealand through the Skilled/Business stream who do not meet a minimum standard of English must prepay for English classes as a condition for receiving a visa. The courses, partially funded by the Tertiary Education Commission (TEC) and endorsed by the New Zealand Qualifications Authority (NZQA), must be taken within five years, or the funds are forfeited. In response to signs that migrants were having difficulty locating courses in smaller locations or that fit their work/family responsibilities, Immigration NZ, together with the TEC launched an online tool to help migrants find a convenient class located near them. The tool is part of the New Zealand Now portal, which offers pre-departure and settling in advice and resources.

Ensuring that migrants get language training early also implies that demand for language training is forecasted efficiently to make sure that spots are readily available and waiting lists are limited. Currently, many OECD countries struggle to provide a sufficient number of courses, which may lead to longer waits (see Table 2.1). One way to reduce wait times is to increase the number of teachers (see Lesson 11). In many countries, strict certification requirements for language teachers, combined with low salaries, have led to a dearth of available educators for integration programmes.

Table 2.1. Timing of access to language training for migrants in OECD and origin countries, 2020 or latest available year

	Average waiting time between enrolment and course placement (length of backlog)	Access to pre-departure language courses	Access for asylum seekers (depending on availability)
Australia	None	No	Yes (except for Illegal Maritime Arrival adults in Community Detention or holding a Bridging Visa type E)
Austria	n.a.	Yes (e-learning)	Yes (asylum seekers with high prospects to remain in Austria)
Belgium	n.a.	No	Yes
Canada	n.a.	No (online self-assessment tool is available pre-departure)	No

	Average waiting time between enrolment and course placement (length of backlog)	Access to pre-departure language courses	Access for asylum seekers (depending on availability)
Chile	/ (no language training provided)	No	No
Colombia	/	No	/
Czech Republic	n.a.	No	No
Denmark	n.a. (but the waiting time between course enrolment and course placement may not exceed 1 month)	No (except for quota refugees)	Yes
Estonia	1 month for welcome programme (longer for other publicly financed language courses)	Yes (e-learning)	Yes
Finland	Approximately 2.5 months after initial assessment (2016)	No (but e-learning tools are available)	Yes
France	18 months within signing the integration contract (CIR)	Yes (in-person courses are not subsidised; e-learning tools are available)	No
Germany	n.a. (but the maximum waiting period is fixed at 3 months)	Yes (including e-learning)	Yes (asylum seekers with good prospects to stay in Germany)
Greece	n.a.	Yes	Yes
Hungary	None	Yes (in Serbia)	Yes
Iceland	/	No	No
Ireland	There is no identified waiting list	No	Yes
Israel	A few days	No	No
Italy	n.a.	Yes (in specific programmes)	Yes
Japan	No waiting time	No	No
Korea	n.a.	Yes	Yes
Latvia	Training must start no later than 1 month after PES client has signed the training voucher	No	Yes
Lithuania	No waiting time	No	No
Luxembourg	n.a. (maximum 3 months as the course offer is trimestral or semesterly)	No (but e-learning tools are available)	Yes
Mexico	n.a.	No	No
Netherlands	n.a.	Yes (e-learning)	Yes
New Zealand	n.a. (some areas of high resettlement have pressure on access to ESOL places)	No	No
Norway	n.a. (2014 target was that 80% start within 6 months)	No	Yes (mandatory for asylum seekers in reception centres)
Poland	n.a.	No	Yes (for asylum seekers who receive social assistance)
Portugal	n.a.	Yes (e-learning)	Yes
Slovak Republic	n.a.	No	Yes
Slovenia	6-12 months (2014)	No	No
Spain	n.a.	No	Yes
Sweden	n.a. (municipalities must provide SFI within a month for those who have an introduction plan and 3 months for others, actual waiting time varies across municipalities, but many offer a spot in a shorter time period than prescribed)	No	Yes
Switzerland	Varies according to canton but	No	Yes (in federal asylum centres and in some

	Average waiting time between enrolment and course placement (length of backlog)	Access to pre-departure language courses	Access for asylum seekers (depending on availability)
	those with large migrant populations have taken measures to increase course availability to avoid backlog.		cantonal centres)
Turkey	n.a.	No	Yes
United Kingdom	n.a.	Yes	Yes
United States	n.a.	Yes (e-learning)	Yes (but not systematically provided)

Note: n.a. = information not available; / = not applicable. See Table 1.1.
Source: OECD questionnaire on language training for adult migrants 2017.

3. Create incentives rather than sanctions to enhance migrants' motivation to learn the host-country language

WHAT and WHY?

Even where immigrants are eligible to participate in language training, participation, let alone successful learning, is not guaranteed. Learning a new language at adult age requires time and commitment – both of which migrants are unlikely to invest unless they actually want or need to learn. Conversely, where expected learning outcomes are sufficiently relevant for an individual, they will find adequate and accessible ways to achieve them. The single most effective way to ensure successful participation in language training is thus to convince migrants of the benefits associated with host-country language proficiency and to help them overcome any doubts they may have about their ability to learn it. Positive, incentive-based policies aimed at enhancing migrants' intrinsic motivation to learn are one way of doing this.

WHO?

Policies aimed at increasing migrants' motivation to participate in language training are particularly important for those migrants who may not independently take the necessary steps to learn the host-country language. Motivation may be different for migrants for whom migration was forced, rather than planned, and policy approaches need to reflect this potential for difference. Adult migrants in particular are instrumentally motivated, often primarily concerned with learning the language that is necessary for them to succeed in specific situations, especially in the labour force. Migrant women with young children or immigrants who settled long ago and have become increasingly distant from the labour market are important target groups in this regard.

HOW?

There are various ways to encourage migrants to learn the host-country language:

- Take action to ensure that migrants understand the benefits of host-language proficiency
- Implement tangible benefits or rewards systems for migrants who attend courses or reach a certain language level

- Where sanctions for non-participation are imposed, consider unintended effects on participants' motivation and ability to learn

Migrants, like all other learners, are more motivated to participate in language training when they are aware of the benefits that language proficiency brings for their daily lives and for the success of subsequent generations. Awareness campaigns illustrating the merits that language proficiency entails for migrants' prospects on the job market and in society at large are an important tool to communicate this message (see Box 3.1). The Italian programme, Vivere e Lavorare in Italia, has experimented with clustering language classes with other complementary services to raise awareness and interest. For example, the "Conoscere per Integrarsi" campaign, run in several municipalities, provided modules in immigration legislation and basic computer science in addition to language. In the past, Germany has used nation-wide billboard advertisement highlighting individual success stories to promote German language learning among immigrants.

Box 3.1. Public campaigns to promote language training amongst immigrants in Estonia and Canada

The Estonian Integration Foundation maintains two different Facebook accounts and organises communication about language learning opportunities in Estonian, English, and Russian, using the various channels that immigrants are likely to use to obtain information, including through its website, news media, social media, and events. In addition to offering free counselling for language learning, the Foundation offers information about services of other agencies and their contacts. Other public services agencies dealing with immigrants are also encouraged to share information about the Foundation's programmes and projects.

Immigration, Refugees, and Citizenship Canada maintains an active YouTube channel with information about the immigration and integration process. The "Language Training Options" video (https://www.canada.ca/en/immigration-refugees-citizenship/news/video/language-training-options.html), is designed to promote awareness of the programme and the benefits of learning English or French. The ability to find a job, participate in the education of children, and to pursue Canadian citizenship are specifically highlighted. The video explains when migrants can access language training, identifies a wide variety of language training options, and directs them to www.canada.ca/new-comerservices. This video and others are available in both of Canada's official languages. In the past, videos have been translated into Spanish, Mandarin Chinese, Hindi, and Arabic (https://www.youtube.com/watch?v=epNZbEuC3YMandfeature=youtu.be).

Another way to enhance migrants' motivation to learn the host-country language is to link completion of language programmes clearly to tangible incentives or rewards, such as more rapid access to residence or citizenship, as is the case in Austria, Denmark, Finland, Germany, and Switzerland. Korea offers additional points on the residency applications of migrants who complete the Korea Immigration & Integration Program (KIIP), which comprises five levels of language in addition to 50 hours of Understanding Korean Society. Some countries, such as Sweden and Denmark have experimented with performance-based rewards in the form of bonus payments to successful learners and/or their municipalities.[5] In Israel, seniority can be earned in public sector positions upon completion of Hebrew courses (Ministry of Aliyah and Integration, 2019). While the Danish scheme is fairly recent and has not been evaluated, an assessment of the Swedish bonus scheme suggested that the latter had only a limited effect on student performance outside of metropolitan areas (Aslund and Engdahl, 2012), and it was discontinued.

Once enrolled in training, incentives must be set to keep learners motivated. The Italian Conoscere per Integrarsi programme offered a certificate of completion if the migrant completed both the language and

IT courses to make the course more attractive. Some countries offer reimbursement of course costs if a certain level is reached within a specified time. For example, Austria reimburses 50% of course costs for migrants able to certify A2-level German within 18 months. As all students, migrants are more likely to succeed when language courses are designed to meet needs-related, transparent, and realistic objectives (compare Lesson 7) and to stimulate further learning through regular evaluations which make progress and remaining needs more apparent (including through self-checks and continuous feedback). Individual migrant integration plans, as developed in many OECD countries, can help meet this need. While individualisation can be a costly investment, there have been demonstrated pedagogical dividends, and costs can be reduced by individual classroom support through use of new technology (Lesson 10).

Box 3.2. Second Chance for Language Learners

Israel implemented a dedicated programme for longer-term residents who have not completed Hebrew studies in the framework of the regular programme for new arrivals. "Second Chance Ulpan" includes four modules of study (speech and verbal expression, listening comprehension, reading comprehension, and writing/written expression), of which participants can chose three, and classes are proposed at various levels with flexible hours.

Norway offers language classes within the context of its "Job Opportunities" programme, which targets migrants who lack a link to the labour market. There is a specific focus on reaching immigrant women who are not dependent on social welfare and, thus, may never have been offered any services. One specific offering within the programme is "job club" conversation groups to improve language proficiency. The programme is divided into three different schemes. Part A-scheme is for immigrant women. In 2019, 75% of participants who had completed the programme in Part A had moved into employment or further education.

The German Integration Course system was originally designed for newcomers, but shortly after its implementation, the course was found to be an efficient instrument for language learning for immigrants who had been living in Germany for a longer time.

While there are good reasons to incentivise migrants to learn the language, forcing them to attend language training by imposing penalties or sanctions may result in resentment or anxiety, and weaken migrants' intrinsic motivation to learn. There is a balance to strike between designing policies that render participation attractive and acknowledging the importance of freedom of choice for motivation. Making access to financial or social benefits conditional upon regular attendance of language training may prove effective if the objectives of such training are based on individual needs and are perceived as transparent and manageable by migrants. However, such conditionality should take into account the individual or family situation of the migrant. For example, a recent investigation conducted for the Danish Ministry of Immigration and Integration found municipalities and languages schools estimate between 50-90% of refugee and family member non-attendance was for legitimate reasons, such as illness (Ankestyrelsen, 2020). Further, quality of education programmes in countries using these "negative" incentives should be carefully monitored to ensure they are adequately tailored to adult needs.

Countries that impose an obligation to reach a certain language level within a prescribed number of years must also carefully consider whether the target level is reasonable. While most OECD countries require a certain level of language proficiency to progress to permanent residency or full citizenship, Austria, Estonia, France, Italy, the Netherlands, and Switzerland impose sanctions earlier (Table 3.2). Policies punishing the failure to pass a test with the loss of a residence permit, the refusal of authorisation to enter a country for the purpose of family reunification, or a fine may be perceived as posing insurmountable obstacles, cause stress, and crowd out migrants' motivation and chances of success (Krumm and Plutzar, 2008). In recognition of the barriers some individuals may face to achieving these targets, Austria, Italy, and the Netherlands offer extensions or exemptions from sanction in certain situations.

"Second chance" integration courses, which exist in Norway and Israel, for example, are a viable alternative for migrants who were not able to acquire sufficient language skills during the normal time limitations, due to illness, family obligations, or lack of course availability. Late integration options provide a way for migrants who have not yet linked to the labour market to build skills and make new steps toward integration (see Box 3.2).

Table 3.1. Compulsory language schemes in OECD countries, 2020 or latest available year

	Obligatory participation	
	Yes/no	If yes: Sanctions used to enforce participation
Australia	No (but may be required as a condition of receiving income support payments)	Financial penalties are possible for failure to attend where mandatory
Austria	Yes	Reduction or loss of social or unemployment benefits according to federal or provincial provisions that apply for insufficient willingness to enter workforce
Belgium	Yes	Administrative fines, or for eligible refugees in Flanders, a loss of social welfare benefits
Canada	No	/
Chile	/	/
Colombia	/	/
Czech Republic	No	/
Denmark	• Yes (asylum seekers, refugees, adult family migrants who arrived through family reunification) • No (accompanying spouses, labour migrants)	Reduction in cash benefits
Estonia	Yes (for refugees and migrants with subsidiary protection status)	Non-participation in language training is taken into account when deciding on the extension of an existing or granting of a new residence permit
Finland	Yes (if part of an integration plan)	Restriction of unemployment benefits for a statutorily defined waiting period
France	Yes (for migrants assigned to language training in the framework of the integration contract CIR)	No
Germany	Yes (for humanitarian migrants, newly arrived adult family migrants and newly arrived labour migrants with insufficient German language skills, in case of special integration needs or for long-term residents who receive social (welfare) benefits)	Sanctions are possible: • Reduction in government benefits and • Refusal to participate can be considered for the decision making on prolonging residence permits for some groups (not humanitarian migrants)
Greece	No	/
Hungary	No	/
Iceland	/	/
Ireland	No	/
Israel	No	/
Italy	No	/
Japan	No	/
Korea	No	/
Latvia	No	/
Lithuania	Yes	Loss of integration support
Luxembourg	Yes (for migrants seeking international protection) No (for other categories)	/

	Obligatory participation	
	Yes/no	**If yes:** **Sanctions used to enforce participation**
Mexico	No	/
Netherlands	No	/
New Zealand	Yes (most immigrants must show knowledge of English or prepay for classes to receive visa)	/
Norway	• Yes (asylum seekers, non-EU labour migrants, refugees and their family members, humanitarian migrants and family members of Norwegians/Nordics) • No (EU nationals)	/
Poland	No	/
Portugal	No	/
Slovak Republic	Yes (for humanitarian migrants who participate in the integration project)	Reduction of financial support for humanitarian migrants who miss more than 25% of the classes
Slovenia	No	/
Spain	No	Migrants who have signed the participation commitment can be excluded from the integration programme if they refuse to participate
Sweden	No, though participation may be associated with receipt of compensation or a social benefit	Potential loss of social benefits
Switzerland	Depends on canton (potential requirement in the "integration contract" between the canton and the migrant)	Yes, but rare, possible sanctions include reduction of social benefits and – under certain rare conditions – non-renewal of residence permit or "retrogradation" from a C permit to a B permit.
Turkey	No	/
United Kingdom	No (but humanitarian migrants are strongly encouraged to participate)	/
United States	No	/

Note: n.a. = information not available; See Table 1.1.
Source: OECD questionnaire on language training for adult migrants 2017.

Table 3.2. Compulsory language schemes in OECD countries, 2020 or latest available year

	Obligation to reach a certain minimum language level within a given time *after* arrival			Level required for permanent residence/ citizenship
	Yes/no	**If yes …**		
		Mandatory minimum level	**Sanctions for not reaching minimum level**	
Australia	No	/	/	Basic English required for citizenship (for applicants under age 60)
Austria	Yes	Within 2 years: • A1 for humanitarian migrants • A2 for adult family migrants and labour migrants	Extension of the 2-year time period or imposition of monetary fine	B1 to obtain long-term residence and citizenship While there is no specified time frame, reaching a B1 level is considered obligatory for humanitarian migrants and beneficiaries of subsidiary protection.
Belgium	No	/	/	A2 in French, Dutch or German for citizenship
Canada	No	/	/	For citizenship, English or French at CLB/NCLC 4 for migrants under the age of

	Obligation to reach a certain minimum language level within a given time *after* arrival			Level required for permanent residence/ citizenship
	Yes/no	If yes …		
		Mandatory minimum level	Sanctions for not reaching minimum level	
				54
Chile	/	/	/	/
Colombia	/	/	/	/
Czech Republic	No	/	/	permanent residence (A1) and citizenship (B1)
Denmark	No	/	/	permanent residence (A2) and citizenship (B1)
Estonia	Yes (for refugees and migrants with subsidiary protection status)	• A1 within 1 year of being granted international protection • A2 within two or 5 years of being granted international protection	• Migrant may have to refund the amounts spent on the provision of language learning • Failure to reach the required language level in the specified time may be taken into account when deciding on the extension of an existing or granting of a new residence permit	Long-term residence and citizenship (B1)
Finland	No	/	/	Equivalent of B1 in Finnish or Swedish for citizenship
France	Yes	A1 for migrants assigned to language training in the framework of the integration contract CIR)	Reaching the A1 is required for award of a multiannual residence permit after 1 year of residence	Permanent residence (A2 after 5 years of residence) and citizenship (B1)
Germany	No	/	/	B1 required for settlement permit in most cases, also for citizenship
Greece	No	/	/	For long-term residency, level B2 or a special certificate (Level A2 plus Greek history and culture) is required. No specific level for citizenship, though knowledge of Greek must be demonstrated in the interview.
Hungary	No	/	/	Basic civics exam in Hungarian for citizenship
Iceland				
Ireland	No	/	/	A test is under consideration for citizenship
Israel	No	/	/	Some Hebrew is needed for a permanent

	Obligation to reach a certain minimum language level within a given time *after* arrival			Level required for permanent residence/ citizenship
	Yes/no	If yes …		
		Mandatory minimum level	Sanctions for not reaching minimum level	
				resident to seek citizenship
Italy	• No (asylum seekers and humanitarian migrants) • Yes (newly arrived labour migrants; newly arrived family migrants commit to but are not legally obliged to reach a level)	A2 level within 2 years of arrival	• Newly arrived migrants cannot complete the "Integration Agreement" with the Italian State if they do not reach a certified linguistic competence at the A2 level • Migrants who do not reach the required level get an extension of 1 year of time	Long-term residence (A2) and citizenship (B1)
Japan	No	/	/	/
Korea	No	/	/	Level 5 Basic Courses required for residency, and Level 5 advanced courses required for citizenship
Latvia	No	/	/	Permanent residence (A2) and citizenship (B1)
Lithuania	Yes (refugees)	A1 in refugee reception centre and A2 when integration continues in the municipality	/	Permanent residence and citizenship (A2)
Luxembourg	Yes	Refugees are obligated to take 120 hours of French (target A1); other migrants who sign the integration contract are expected to reach the A1 level in one of the 3 official languages within 2 years	/	For citizenship, A2 spoken Luxembourgish, B1 listening
Mexico	No	/	/	
Netherlands	• Yes (humanitarian migrants and most types of family migrants) • No (highly skilled migrants, entrepreneurs,	A2[i]	Administrative fine for migrants who do not pass the exam within 3 years and can (except humanitarian migrants) face withdrawal of a temporary residence permit (exemptions are made for medical	Permanent residence (A2)

	Obligation to reach a certain minimum language level within a given time *after* arrival			Level required for permanent residence/ citizenship
	Yes/no	If yes ...		
		Mandatory minimum level	**Sanctions for not reaching minimum level**	
	and immigrants with a residence permit based on employment, or their dependent family members)		reasons)	
New Zealand	No	/	/	
Norway	No[ii]	/	/	For migrants age 18-67, permanent residence (having completed language training or A2 + civics test) and citizenship (B1 oral + civics test in Norwegian)
Poland	No (though progress is expected within framework of integration programme)	/	/	Permanent residence (B1)
Portugal	No	/	/	Permanent residence (A2)
Slovak Republic	No (but planned for humanitarian migrants)	/	/	
Slovenia	No	/	/	A2-B1 for citizenship
Spain	No	/	/	
Sweden	No	/	/	Requirement agreed but not yet implemented
Switzerland	Yes (a specific level can be defined in the "integration contract" between the canton and the refugee)	Minimum level is fixed for family migrants	Sanctions depend on overall integration efforts (not only language learning) and include non-issuance or non-renewal of residence permit (B permit)	Settled migrant (C permit) requires A1 written and A2 oral in language of place of residence; citizenship requires B1 oral and A2 written
Turkey	No	/	/	
United Kingdom	No	/	/	Permanent residence (B1)
United States	No	/	/	English proficiency required for citizenship (with age + length of residency exceptions)

Notes: n.a. = information not available; See Table 1.1.

[i.] The target level in the Netherlands will change from A2 to B1 effective July 2021, with an exception for those who are unlikely to be able to meet it.

[ii.] Norway's new Integration Act, implemented 1 January 2021, creates a benchmark for language courses dependent upon educational background. Implementation of the noted requirement of a B1 level for citizenship is planned for 2021.

Source: OECD questionnaire on language training for adult migrants 2017.

4. Consider affordability when developing financing models to ensure costs are not an obstacle

WHAT and WHY?

In order to be effective and equitable, language courses should be available to all immigrants in need who are expected to remain in the country – independent of their financial means. However, language schemes tend to be expensive, particularly at the top and bottom end of the skills scale. Training for illiterate adults is the costliest type of programme, which may pay off only in the long run when the children of illiterate participants benefit from their parents' learning in terms of higher educational attainment. Not surprisingly then, some newcomers, low-income groups, and unemployed migrants cannot afford the high upfront costs for private language training. Most OECD countries have responded to this by introducing publicly funded language programmes with little or no fees for eligible participants to guarantee that costs do not prevent eligible learners from participating.

WHO?

Unemployed migrants often have access to financial support from the public employment service, enabling them to participate in language training. However, those in need who are not looking for a job and/or not eligible for benefits would also benefit from access to subsidised language programmes.

HOW?

Across the OECD, the extent to which language training is subsidised differs (see Table 4.1), and countries have experimented with various financing tools:

- Language course can be free of charge or a means-tested benefit
- Migrants can access courses through a deposit system
- Migrants can be offered loans to pay for language courses
- Results-based financing can be arranged with providers

There is no clear-cut answer as to whether courses should be free of charge, and in some cases, budgeting constraints make this impossible. Offering free courses may also lead to the perception that they do not have value. However, many OECD countries consider language training a public good, which should be free of charge for eligible learners. This approach is prevalent for instance in the Nordic countries, Belgium, Canada, France, Italy, Portugal, and Slovenia (see Box 3.2). Some countries also reimburse participants' transportation costs. Alternatively, language training can be seen as a means-tested opportunity where learners pay only what they can. This generally implies that fees are waived or symbolic for basic and intermediate courses for all unemployed and low-income learners. Any other fees are set at levels that are not dissuasive for learners who can pay. Fully or partly means-tested schemes are currently in place in the United Kingdom, Germany, Luxembourg, Estonia, Hungary, Austria and the Czech Republic. In Australia, which has free English language training for most new arrivals in need, there is a higher visa fee (around AUD 5 000, depending on the category) for spouses and dependents lacking functional English. Similarly, in New Zealand, most visa applicants must meet minimum language requirements or pre-purchase English tuition. The cost of tuition ranges from NZD 1 735 to 6 795, depending on initial English levels.

Requiring migrants to make some up-front investment in their language training may provide an incentive to complete a course. New Zealand has seen increased uptake year over year since implementing the prepayment policy. As of December 2018, 59% of migrants with Pre-purchased English Language Tuition (PELT) entitlements ending in 2018 had used all or part of their English for Speakers of other Languages (ESOL) tuition (New Zealand Government, 2019). However, a deposit system may be a more effective way to promote migrant commitment to the programme while at the same time offering a public good. From 1995-98, New Zealand had a language bond, requiring spouses and dependents to pay a certain amount that was reimbursed if they managed to acquire the required minimum level of English language within a year of arrival. Currently, Germany will reimburse 50% of costs if migrants pass the end-of-course examination within two years. Austria uses a similar incentive structure (see Lesson 3). Both Denmark and the Czech Republic (for some courses) experimented with a deposit that is returned upon completion of the course. The deposit for Czech courses may be forfeit in the case of unexcused absences. Denmark introduced its deposit scheme in 2017 before changing to a fee-paying model for self-supporting migrants in 2018. As of July 2020, the country has returned to a deposit scheme for self-supporting migrants at a slightly higher monetary amount (DKK 2 000 per module compared to DKK 1 250 per module in 2017). Students receive vouchers that state the maximum timeframe in which to complete each module. Migrants in the integration programme do not have to pay a deposit to access free Danish classes.

In addition, some countries provide no-interest or reduced-interest loans for individuals and businesses that engage in advanced trainings with high payoffs. In contrast to grants, loans are appropriate for programmes with an expected high financial return on investment for the migrant and are usually used by individuals with high socio-economic potential or tertiary-level education. Although rarely applied in this context to date, loans could also be used to finance advanced occupation-specific language training for high-income professions, such as medicine and engineering. Wherever fees are charged, or loans are the only available option for prospective learners, it is important to monitor for signs of under-investment due to an unwillingness or inability to pay. An evaluation of Estonia's integration programme revealed that only 5-9% of migrants were willing or able to pay more than 80% of costs of language courses. Between 33-39% of respondents were unwilling to pay anything at all. Evaluators determined that discontinuing state funding would undermine Estonia's integration goals (Centar, 2018).

Financing models can also be used to apply incentives for performance by providers. Denmark has used a results-based financing system in which providers are paid half the money prior to the course and half after the individual migrant has passed the course exam. An evaluation showed that financial incentives encourage service providers to contribute to more efficient and individually oriented tuition (Ramboll, 2007b). To ensure that slower learners are not lost in such a system, funders should consider a sliding scale of financial incentives according to the knowledge acquisition level of migrants (i.e. higher reimbursements for cases that require more investment).

To implement incentive structures, evaluations need to be included, and the capacity to manage bonuses and reimbursements must be matched to administrative systems. A centrally organised support function is needed to provide help and information regarding the benchmarking. Even though national budgets may not reflect the whole landscape given the role of municipal or state/provincial governments in funding programmes in some countries, it is clear that overall, language training represents the bulk of government expenditures on immigrant integration in most OECD countries. To reduce budgetary burden, multiple public and private stakeholders should be encouraged to contribute. Employers can be asked to subsidise language training costs for sponsored labour migrants and on-the-job trainings, and professional bodies, vocational training programmes, and private higher education institutions can contribute to financing advanced and occupation-specific language training.

Box 4.1. Subsidies for language programmes

Israel's Absorption Basket (Sal Klita) offers financial assistance for Jewish newcomers covering their expenses during six months of Hebrew courses (ulpan) and their rent for the first year. The benefit can be combined with an additional income support for the unemployed or vocational training students. An online calculator allows users to calculate the size of their benefit, which depends on their age and family situation.

In Finland, Norway, and Sweden, in the broader framework of the introduction programmes of which language training is a key component, language learners receive financial assistance that is conditional upon course attendance and complementary with paid work. In Sweden, participants in the introduction plan are entitled to an individual introduction benefit covering their expenses for up to two years. Based on the learner's introduction plan, the public employment service determines the size of the benefit (approx. EUR 35 per day) and costs related to children and housing. The amount is not affected by the income of other household members in order to create stronger incentives for both spouses to learn Swedish and prepare for work. As with study grants, the benefit can be lost due to non-attendance, but can be combined with work at a reduced rate for six months. The requirements are similar in Finland, where means-tested assistance (approx. EUR 33 per day, paid five days per week including holidays) covers the expenses for participants in the introduction plan for up to five years. The amount equates to (and replaces) the unemployment benefits for the unemployed. In Norway, refugee learners and family migrants are entitled to an introduction benefit for the duration of their introduction programme, subject to attendance. The amount of the benefit is taxable and equivalent to twice the level of national insurance. The benefit can be combined with (i.e. does not replace) other benefits (e.g. unemployment, sickness/disability, maternity/child benefits) or with work outside of the programme.

Table 4.1. Costs for publicly financed language programmes in OECD countries, latest available year

	Fully or partially subsidised language courses (incl. e-learning)	Total budgeted expenditures	Overall per participant per hour costs paid to provider (in Euros)	Fee paid by participant per hour (in Euros)
Australia	Yes	AUS 225 698 000 (approx. EUR 143.2 million) incl. tuition cost, childcare and counselling fees (FY 2018/19)	n.a.	Free of charge
Austria	Yes (and e-learning)	Federal Chancellery: EUR 32 million (01/2019 – 03/2021) PES: EUR 61.3 million (2019) and EUR 67.8 million (2020)	n.a.	Courses organised by the Austrian Integration Fund and PES are free of charge. Integration agreement: Generally, participants pay course costs, yet can apply for partial reimbursement of the obligatory Module 1 (up to 50% of the costs) if they successfully pass Module 1 within the first 18 months of their stay
Belgium	Yes (e-learning for family migrants coming to Flanders/Brussels)	EUR 8 386 460 in Wallonia EUR 8 000 000 for francophone Brussels	n.a.	Free of charge for participants involved in an integration programme (sometimes annual

	Fully or partially subsidised language courses (incl. e-learning)	Total budgeted expenditures	Overall per participant per hour costs paid to provider (in Euros)	Fee paid by participant per hour (in Euros)
		EUR 300 000 for integration programme courses in the German-speaking community (2020)		enrolment fees of EUR 15-42 for course material), except in Flemish Region, where fees are EUR 1.5 per lesson (EUR 180 maximum for lessons and test)
Canada	Yes (remote placement assessments and online/distance training options also available at no cost to the client; Quebec reimburses costs for language course abroad)	CAD 261.4 million (approx. EUR 178 million) federal funding for language assessment and training (FY2019-20) In Quebec, CAD 170.3 million (approx. EUR 116.5) (FY2019-20)	n.a.	Free of charge for permanent residents and refugees (federal level) In Quebec, financial assistance is available (CAD 188 per week for full-time courses and CAD 15 per day for part-time courses).
Chile	No	/	/	/
Colombia	/	/	/	/
Czech Republic	Yes	n.a.	n.a.	n.a.
Denmark	Yes	Approx. EUR 170 million (2018)	n.a.	Free of charge for persons covered by the Integration Act. Workers and students must pay a refundable DKK 2 000 deposit to start training.
Estonia	Yes	EUR 6 789 200 for total Welcoming Programme (until 2023)	EUR 5.6 + VAT (EUR 450 + VAT in total per participant)	Free of charge
Finland	Yes (e-learning is not systematic, but available through Helsinki City, infofinland.fi, others)	EUR 51 million (2019)	EUR 35 (per student per day in 2019)	Free of charge
France	Yes	EUR 247.9 million for integration contract activities including language training + 53.91 million for longer-term (2020)	n.a.	Free of charge
Germany	Yes	Approx. EUR 1 billion (integration courses and vocational courses)	EUR 3.90 (integration course); EUR 4.14 (vocational course) (2020) Beginning 2021: EUR 4.40 (integration course); EUR 4.64 (vocational course)	EUR 2.20 (2021), except for certain exempt migrants. May be reimbursed 50% upon successful completion within 2 years EUR 2.62 (2021) for vocational language courses. Free for persons without employment
Greece	No (except reception centres)	Approx. EUR 150 000 (2018); Approx. EUR 210 000 (2019). For courses in 4 Migrant Integration Centres – ESF	n.a.	Free of charge
Hungary	Yes (e-learning and face-to-face courses in Serbia)	EUR 173 675 (01/2014-06/2015)	EUR 2.70 (2015)	Free of charge
Iceland	Yes	/	/	/
Ireland	Yes	/	/	/
Israel	Yes (Israeli teachers teach Hebrew and provide information about Israel in Jewish	/	/	/

	Fully or partially subsidised language courses (incl. e-learning)	Total budgeted expenditures	Overall per participant per hour costs paid to provider (in Euros)	Fee paid by participant per hour (in Euros)
	schools and the local Jewish communities abroad)			
Italy	Yes	EUR 18 973 862 (05/2014-06/2015)	n.a.	Free of charge
Japan	Yes	EUR 4 074 444 (FY 2015)	n.a.	Free of charge
Korea	Yes (e-learning and face-to-face classes through the King Sejong Institutes)	EUR 5 164 670 (FY 2019)	n.a.	Free of charge
Latvia	Yes	EUR 1 427 666,62 (2019)	The sum of the voucher not exceeding EUR 360	Free of charge for eligible participants at Public Employment Service and in asylum-seeker accommodation centres
Lithuania	Yes	EUR 800 000 (2019)	/	/
Luxembourg	Yes	EUR 1.5 million (2012-15)	EUR 4	EUR 0.20 per course (reduced cost); EUR 3 per cost (regular cost)
Mexico	No (but e-learning options available)	/	/	Refugees pay a lower rate
Netherlands	Yes (e-learning/self-learning package)	EUR 61 million	n.a.	Loan-based but humanitarian migrants who pass the exam within the established period do not have to pay back the loan
New Zealand	Yes	EUR 21.9 million (2014)	n.a.	Cost is dependent on level
Norway	Yes (and e-learning)	EUR 99.8 million (2021)	EUR 177 (2019)	Participation fee varies
Poland	Yes	/	/	/
Portugal	Yes (and e-learning)	EUR 263 093 (2017-18)	EUR 3.00 (2017-18)	Free of charge
Slovak Republic	No (but e-learning options)	/	/	/
Slovenia	Yes	EUR 416 900 (FY2014)	EUR 2.9	Free of charge
Spain	No	EUR 1 397 407 for total integration programme (2014)	/	Free of charge
Sweden	Yes (with residence permit)	SEK 3 793 887 (approx. EUR 358 366) for sfi (2019)	SEK 51 900 (approx. EUR 4 902) per year	Free of charge
Switzerland	Yes (not e-learning)	EUR 64 million (2018)	/	5 CHF per lesson in some cantons, free in others
Turkey	Yes	/	/	/
United Kingdom	Yes	/	/	Free for unemployed immigrants receiving benefits
United States	Yes (and e-learning)	On federal level: USD 657 million (approx. EUR 560,4 million) for appropriations under AEFLA (Adult Education and Family Literacy Act), plus additional funding for refugee programmes[i] (FY2020)	n.a.	Government subsidises classes (and other resettlement services) through grants to specifically identified partner organisations and centres for adult education

Note: n.a. = information not available; / = not applicable; See Table 1.1.

[i.] In the United States., language provision for refugees is funded separately under Refugee Support Services. This USD 270 million appropriation includes employment related services and specialised programmes in addition to English as a Second Language.

Source: OECD questionnaire on language training for adult migrants 2017.

5. Make language training flexible and compatible with job-search, work, education and daily life constraints

WHAT and WHY?

Challenges related to access, motivation, and affordability of language training are compounded by the fact that many adult migrants face personal and/or work-related constraints to attend courses regularly at a fixed time of the day, in a particular location, or during a given period of the year. Indeed, according to a survey from 2012,[6] lack of time is self-identified as the main obstacle preventing immigrants from learning the host-country language. Conversely, immigrants who are enrolled in full-time language programmes have often no time to work or look for a job. As a consequence, labour market integration is delayed and lock-in effects are likely, as employers tend to penalise candidates with long absences from the labour market. To overcome these challenges and facilitate migrants' ability to fit language learning into their daily lives, it is crucial to allow for flexibility in course schedules, locations, and learning formats.

WHO?

Some migrant groups are particularly affected by rigid training schedules and inaccessible settings. Migrants with low income and recent arrivals, for example, may find it particularly difficult to participate in language programmes that prevent them from pursuing a regular job, as they often require a fixed income to support their family, secure residence rights, and obtain permission for family reunification. Another group that is likely to suffer from scheduling conflicts are migrant parents, and particularly immigrant mothers with small children, who may have fewer childcare or babysitting options, due to financial constraints and limited social and extended family networks in the country.

HOW?

Policy attempts to address this issue take several forms (see Table 5.1):

- Provide courses in easily accessible locations and environments
- Anticipate the needs of migrant women with small children
- Consider flexibility of course timing to account for work or other obligations

In order to be effective, programme designers must anticipate, monitor, and respond to a wide range of potential obstacles. First, the setting of courses needs to be chosen carefully. Preferably the location is well known by learners, easily accessible, and well equipped for language learning. Options include community centres, libraries, immigrant associations, or the school of learners' children. While vocational and higher education institutions may be attractive locations for students and labour migrants, they may not necessarily be the most accessible and inviting locations for some family migrants and low-income learners. In this case, informal learning options should be available, allowing language acquisition at places where the target group already interacts and feels comfortable. An example of such a programme is "Bazaar: Learn and Exchange at the Market Place," which ran from 2013-2018. The project, which was funded by the European Commission, organised language training for adult migrants in Bulgaria, Germany, Italy, Portugal, and the United Kingdom in informal, every-day settings, such as the marketplace, local supermarkets, gymnasiums, or children's schools.

Many countries are specifically concerned with increasing participation of immigrant women, particularly those with childcare responsibilities.[7] In response, several countries now provide courses targeted toward women or mothers. The benefit of gender homogenous courses is subject to debate, particularly when considering social integration. A number of countries avoid such courses out of concern that they send a negative signal regarding gender equality. Other countries have taken the opposite stance based on the view, for which there is some evidence, that this approach increases female participation in language courses.[8] In practice, where they exist, courses specifically for women are still the exception rather than the rule. In Germany, 6 313 migrants participated in language courses for Parents and Women in the first half of 2019, 90% of whom were women. At the same time, an overwhelming majority of women participated in the general Integration Course (75 166 women, or 57% of enrolment in the general course). Germany takes the additional step of advertising that its courses for women are also taught exclusively by women. The City of Vienna, Austria reported that over 8 000 women participated in its "Mom Learns German" programme between 2006 and 2017.

One promising alternative to gender-specific courses are courses that address gender-specific barriers. Courses such as Germany's courses for parents, designed to accommodate for childcare obligations and inform about child-specific issues, are one such example. While most participants are women and gender-specific needs may be addressed, they are not framed as gender-separated courses. Some countries have innovated by organising language training at childcare facilities, for example by allowing mothers and children to learn together, also solves the issue of free and accessible childcare during the course. Flanders (Belgium) launched a pilot programme for women with children in 2016, with several language modules centred on communication relevant to parents and accredited childcare provided onsite. Alternatively, some countries, including Canada and the United Kingdom, have introduced place-based learning (i.e. learning can be organised at home if migrants feel more comfortable). The French Ministry of Interior and Ministry of National Education have partnered to develop the programme "Open the School to Parents for the Success of Children (OEPRE), which offers French courses at the school where the migrant's child is enrolled, including a module on understanding the school's needs and expectations for its students and parents. In its first year (school year 2017-2018), the 460 workshops were offered for around 17 parents each. 84% of participating parents were women.

While migrants pursuing educational opportunities may benefit most from part-time, evening, or weekend language courses, 'on-the-job' training is usually the most attractive option for working migrants (see Lesson 6). Wherever 'on-the-job' training is not available, language programmes should be sufficiently flexible to allow immigrants to work on the side. If full-time formats are the only available option, courses should not surpass a critical number of hours beyond which there is no additional impact on the employment prospects of immigrants (OECD, 2007). There is a further option for learners with Information and Communication Technology (ICT) literacy.

ICT-based learning programmes (see Lesson 10) typically target young people, technology affine migrants, and the tertiary educated and are most effective when focused on simple-to-use and frequently used ICT tools, such as mobile phones, MP3 players, TV, and well-known internet media.

To facilitate migrants' ability to reconcile language training with daily life constraints, countries ideally offer a multitude of different learning formats. This is for instance the case in Australia, Canada, and New Zealand, where learners can choose from a broad variety of learning options, ranging from self-study materials to fully teacher-led courses (see Box 5.1).

Box 5.1. Flexible language courses in OECD settlement countries

Australia, Canada and New Zealand offer a flexible set of language training options, usually including part-time, evening, and weekend courses, as well as distance and ICT-based learning, one-on-one tutoring, free child-care, transportation subsidies, and continuous intake to avoid long waiting lists. Migrants who cannot attend classroom-based formats (e.g. because of shift work, illness or lack of local courses, transportation, or child-care) are offered free one-on-one lessons for a few hours per week with a trained instructor or community volunteer. These programmes are called Volunteer Home Tutor Schemes in Australia and English Language Partners in New Zealand. Learners may also follow an online or correspondence course such as Canada's Language Instruction for Newcomers to Canada (LINC) Home Study/Cours de langue pour les immigrants au Canada (CLIC) en ligne, available in several Canadian provinces. The latter cost much less than classroom-based learning formats, but learners progress more slowly due to limited training hours and availability of volunteers.

Table 5.1. Flexible options for language training in OECD countries, 2020 or latest available year

	Government co-funded website providing e-language training	Evening facilities for language training	Childcare options
Australia	Yes	Yes	Yes
Austria	Yes	Yes	Yes
Belgium	Yes (Wallonia – not specifically targeted to migrants) No (Brussels-Capital Region)	No (Wallonia) Yes (Brussels-Capital Region)	No
Canada	Yes	Yes	Yes
Chile	No	No	No
Colombia	/	/	/
Czech Republic	Yes	Yes	Yes
Denmark	No (may be offered by provider)	Yes	n.a. (but in general all children in Denmark benefit from guaranteed day-care availability in their municipality)
Estonia	Yes	Yes	No
Finland	Yes	No (but training providers can provide classes to targeted groups at a time suitable for them)	Yes (organised by municipalities, except for groups for stay-at-home parents, where the service provider is responsible for provision of babysitting)
France	Yes	No	No
Germany	Yes	Yes	Yes
Greece	No	Yes	No (not systematic but in some cases)
Hungary	No	No	No
Iceland	/	/	/
Ireland	No	Yes	Yes
Israel	Yes	Yes (for migrants who start to work after being granted their status)	No
Italy	Yes	No (not systematic but in some locations)	No (not systematic but in some locations)
Japan	No	Yes	No
Korea	Yes	Yes	No

	Government co-funded website providing e-language training	Evening facilities for language training	Childcare options
Latvia	Yes	No (not systematic, but depends on the service provider)	No
Lithuania	No	Yes	Yes
Luxembourg	Yes (for Luxembourgish)	Yes	No
Mexico	Yes	Yes	No
Netherlands	No	Yes	Yes (depends on the service provider)
New Zealand	No	No (depends on the service provider)	No (but some providers have childcare facilities on site and subsidised childcare is available for children from age 3 onwards)
Norway	Yes	Yes	No (but migrants benefit from national scheme of free core child care hours)
Poland	No	Yes	Yes
Portugal	Yes	Yes	Yes
Slovak Republic	Yes (supported by European Commission)	No	No
Slovenia	Yes	Yes	No
Spain	Yes	Yes	No
Sweden	Yes (depends on the service provider)	Yes	No (but all children have the right to pre-school)
Switzerland	No	Yes	Yes
Turkey	No	Yes	No
United Kingdom	No (depends on the service provider)	No (depends on the service provider)	No (depends on the service provider)
United States	Yes	Yes	No (not systematic but in some states)

Note: n.a. = information not available; See Table 1.1.
Source: OECD questionnaire on language training for adult migrants 2017.

Table 5.2. Timing and duration of language training in OECD countries, 2020 or latest available year

	Number of hours available to average participants (may be fee-based)	Number of publicly funded hours available for humanitarian migrants	Number of hours available to learners with special needs (e.g. illiterate, traumatised, etc.)
Australia	No limit (as of April 2021)	No limit (as of April 2021)	No limit (as of April 2021)
Austria	300	600	/
Belgium	240 (Flanders) 400 (Wallonia) 150 – 1 350 (Brussels-Capital Region) Min. 360 (German-speaking community)	600 (Flanders and Brussels-Capital Region)	480 (Slower learners – Flanders) 250 – 1 350 (Slower learners – Brussels-Capital Region)
Canada	No limit	No limit	
Chile	/	/	/
Colombia	/	/	/
Czech Republic	210	400	/
Denmark	No predetermined number of hours (within 42 months)	Average 15 hr/week over 5 years	/
Estonia	80	300	/
Finland	2100 (60 credit units)	2100	40 additional credit units (nonliterate)
France	400	400	600 (nonliterate)
Germany	600 (plus 100-hour orientation course); 400 for intensive programme (plus 30-hour orientation course)	n.a.	• 900 hours (migrants with special needs or nonliterate) (plus 100-hour orientation course) • An additional 300 hours are available for any migrant unable to reach the language goal (B1)

	Number of hours available to average participants (may be fee-based)	Number of publicly funded hours available for humanitarian migrants	Number of hours available to learners with special needs (e.g. illiterate, traumatised, etc.)
			in the allocated number of hours
Greece	n.a.	n.a.	n.a.
Hungary	n.a.		
Iceland			
Ireland			
Israel	500		
Italy	100		
Japan	/	/	/
Korea	485		
Latvia	120-150	120	
Lithuania			
Luxembourg	60 (3 courses)	120 hours	
Mexico	126		
Netherlands	240	No limit	
New Zealand		No limit	
Norway	Based on individual needsⁱ	Based on individual needs	Based on individual needs
Poland		No limit	
Portugal	300	No limit	
Slovak Republic			
Slovenia	180	300-400	
Spain	280-420		
Sweden	No limit	No limit	
Switzerland	300-600	Depends on canton	
Turkey	120-180		
United Kingdom	6-12 weeks	12 months (8 hr/week minimum)	
United States	/	/	/

Note: n.a. = information not available; See Table 1.1.

i. The new Integration Act in Norway, implemented 1 January 2021, removes the requirement to complete a number of hours of language training. Instead, each individual shall be asked to achieve a minimum level in Norwegian. This level is the participant's Norwegian Goal. The indicative minimum level is B1 in all language skills (oral, listening, writing and reading), but it will be differentiated based on the individual's prior formal education. There may also be differentiation in the goal across the different language skills.

Source: OECD questionnaire on language training for adult migrants 2017.

6. Integrate language with vocational training and co-operate with employers

WHAT and WHY?

Many language courses designed for everyday life are not particularly relevant or sufficient for the realities of the labour market. Few courses available today model relevant workplace interactions or teach the relevant vocabulary migrants will use on the job. Many adult migrants may be demotivated to continue language courses perceived to be only somewhat relevant when they could be job-seeking, leading to difficulties integrating in other areas of life. Vocation-specific language training – ideally provided on the job – is an effective tool to circumvent such problems, allowing migrants to build work-related language skills while gathering work experience in the host country. Indeed, combining language instruction and vocational training has proven more effective than separate, parallel or sequential trainings in terms of future labour market inclusion. It also appears that learners advance more quickly and are more motivated to complete their programme successfully when the curriculum builds on their career goals and allows participants to apply skills to real-life situations (Roberts, 2003; Chenven, 2004; Delander et al., 2005; Friedenberg, 2014). On-the-job language training may also help address employers' reticence about immigrants' language qualifications. Co-operation with employers can increase their understanding of what the language levels actually mean and assure them that successful learners have in fact acquired the language skills required for the job (Chiswick and Miller, 2009).

WHO?

To date, the number of immigrants benefiting from vocation-specific language training in OECD countries is still limited due to the fact that such training is costly and difficult to organise. The number of immigrants interested in a particular occupation or sector is often too low for providers to consider it worthwhile to develop the capacity to organise trainings regularly. At the same time, the number of employers willing to accommodate language learning in the workplace is limited, which means that language and vocational training are often offered in parallel by separate providers and funded by stakeholders with different objectives.

HOW?

Despite its costs and organisational challenges, vocational language training is gradually spreading across OECD countries in different forms:

- Vocational language courses tailored to specific high-need occupations
- Courses focused on general workplace scenarios or job interviews
- "On-the-job" sessions in partnership with specific employers
- In connection with Active Labour Market Policies and job placement

Vocation-specific courses have been embraced by Austria, Australia, Belgium, Denmark, Germany, Israel, Luxembourg, Portugal, and Sweden (see Table 6.1). Others, such as Lithuania, have made the addition of vocational language training a part of recent plans for action on integration. However, only a few countries have thus far been able to deliver work-related trainings in a wide range of occupations. This is the case, for example, in Portugal, where technical, sector-specific Portuguese courses are offered in retailing, hospitality, beauty care, construction, and civil engineering. Portugal has also recently authorised Qualification Centres to host these courses so that less-qualified trainees may gain easier access to skills and qualification reinforcement programmes onsite. Likewise, Sweden provides specific language schemes for certain occupations such as teachers, academics, engineers, economists, lawyers, social/human resources personnel, systems specialists, health care workers, entrepreneurs, bakers, craftsmen, and bus and truck drivers. Germany has implemented special vocational training courses for health, retail, and technical professions and is currently testing courses for apprentices in craft trades.

Most countries offering vocational language training have rather opted for a general course on workplace language needs. This reflects the difficulty of developing and implementing highly technical language courses for specific vocations when the number of interested migrants is low. In these general courses, migrants would benefit from a degree of individual attention within the course, through breakout sessions that are vocation specific or through differentiated vocabulary study. This can be facilitated in-class through effective implementation of ICT (see Lesson 10).

To expand the availability of on-the-job and vocational language training offers, there is also the option of engaging with specific employers or sectors. Employers can be encouraged in information sessions or in one-on-one meetings to cover or reduce the organisational costs associated with vocational language training, for example by providing classroom space or allowing employees to participate in language learning during working hours (see Box 6.1). Training can be organised independently by employers, trade unions, or structurally through state-sponsored language programmes. In state-sponsored programmes, vocation-specific training can be provided as a specific track for learners (often in the framework of bridging offers) in certain professions with particular employers, or as a second step for all working-age learners who have attained the basic proficiency level required for their profession. On-the-job programmes help employers better understand the needed language competency, and employers can, in turn, become good partners in development of targeted language programmes. The Canadian province of Quebec has developed partnerships with employers and unions in addition to institutional actors and the community to strengthen on-the-job training to meet the needs of migrant employees. Quebec has also worked to create a reference framework to determine the minimum linguistic requirements for varying professions and trades.

On-the-job programmes remain rare, with companies citing the administrative burden as a disadvantage to implementation. Some countries have, thus, explored other solutions. In Sweden, the Sfi-Yrkesvux programme combines Swedish courses and language support combined with studies for a profession in the adult education system. Language support is continued during related internships or work placement. Luxembourg has instituted a programme called "Linguistic Leave" for workers who want to improve their Luxembourgish. The migrant's employer must approve the leave, but any decision to deny the application must be justified. The employee is entitled to up to 200 hours of paid leave to attend language training, and the employer is reimbursed 50% of the compensatory benefit by the state. Language teachers have evaluated the relevance of industry-specific company-organised programmes positively compared to traditional courses (Ramboll, 2020).

Box 6.1. Vocational language training in Germany, Finland, and Norway

In 2016, Germany put in place a wide-reaching new system of free vocation-specific language courses, entitled "German for professional purposes". The courses target foreign-born unemployed, job- or apprenticeship-seekers and their children who have completed mandatory schooling and intermediate German language training (CEFR B1). Migrants in employment are eligible for the course as well, but they must pay 50% of the cost if their income is above a certain threshold. Courses teach German for the job market and in some instances for specific professions, including German language skills required for the recognition of foreign qualifications (e.g. medicine). They can include site visits. Vocational language training is offered through level C2 and can start under B1 for those who not yet attained a B1 level of German after attending an integration course. Germany has also taken an innovative approach in tackling difficulties associated with co-ordination, as the vocation-specific language training together with the integration course constitute the comprehensive programme ('Gesamtprogramm Sprache') that is administered by the Federal Office for Migration and Refugees and funded both by the Ministry of the Interior (integration courses) and the Ministry of Labour (vocation-specific courses).

The Federal Office for Migration and Refugees (BAMF) has also successfully partnered with large companies to provide sector-specific language courses for migrants. Working with Deutsche Telekom, BAMF set up a virtual classroom to reach refugees working at various corporate locations nationwide (2-3 per site). In 2017, through this programme, 100 refugees were able to access both language and on-the-job IT training.

As part of the Finnish Integration Plan, local Public Employment Service Offices (under the Ministry of Employment and Economy) provide language courses that include a "working life period," during which migrants work at a Finnish worksite. The office also provides support services for companies that employ migrants, including pay subsidies to cover hiring costs and training time. While community coaching is one aspect of this programme the employers can also seek funding for Workplace Finnish or Workplace Swedish, and the programme is tailored to the needs and language proficiency of the employees. Duration of the programme, delivery method (in person or distance), group size, and time of course offering are all negotiable. The employer pays 30-50% of the training costs, and the rest is covered.

Skills Norway, which is responsible for implementation and development of pedagogical approaches related to the teaching of Norwegian to adult immigrants, offers several options for vocational learning. In addition to language courses that address workplace situations, Skills Norway offers a job internship placement. While limited resources do not allow for provision of on-the-job language training, public or private entities that seek to provide training to workers can apply for Kompetansepluss (Skills Plus) funding in order to organise their own course. Certain Norwegian language training providers independently advertise their assistance to employers in applying for the funding and organising courses.

Another way to enhance the effectiveness of language training with regards to labour market integration and to strengthen on-the-job and vocational language training options is to involve actors responsible for Active Labour Market Policies (ALMPs) in the design and delivery of language programmes. In co-operation with employers and professional bodies, ALMP providers can develop curricula, teaching material, teacher training, and certifications for integrated language and vocational training and link language training to out-of-class activities, such as mentoring and job placements schemes. Australia is among the OECD countries that pioneered on-the-job language training. Beginning in 1991, Australian authorities provided funding to employers for training their workers in 'Workplace English Language and

Literary' (WELL). While this programme has ended, other government-funded courses are now in place. Australia's 'Adult Migrant English Programme' (AMEP) also includes a 'Settlement Language Pathways to Employment and Training' (SLPET), entitling participants to up to 200 hours of vocation-specific language tuition and up to 80 hours of work placements.

Table 6.1. Implementation of Vocational Language Training in OECD countries

	Vocational (General Workplace) Language Courses Available	Vocational Language Courses Targeting Specific Job Categories	On-the-Job Language Courses Available
Australia	Yes	/	Yes
Austria	Yes	Yes (care workers, early childhood education, production and stock, tourism, business, and nursing staff)	No
Belgium	Yes	Yes	No
Canada	Yes (in some locations; not systematically)	No at the federal level. Quebec offers part-time courses for law, administration, applied sciences, health, and tourism. A course for cooking/restauranteurs is in development.	Yes (in some locations; not systematically)
Chile	/	/	/
Colombia	/	/	/
Czech Republic	Yes	No	No
Denmark	Yes	/	Yes (project in pilot form)
Estonia	No	No	No
Finland	Yes	Yes	Yes
France	No	No	No
Germany	Yes	Yes (medical, commercial, trade and technology)	Yes (not systematically)
Greece	No	No	No
Hungary	No	No	No
Iceland	/	/	/
Ireland	No	No	No
Israel	Yes	Yes (hi-tech sector, engineering, medical)	Yes (kibbutz work programme)
Italy	Yes	Yes (in some locations)	No
Japan	Yes	Yes (nursing)	No
Korea	/	/	/
Latvia	No	No	Yes (80 hours for refugees and those with subsidiary protection)
Lithuania	No	No	No (although possible under a Competence Voucher programme)
Luxembourg	No	No	No
Mexico	No	No	No
Netherlands	Yes (in some cases)	No	Yes (not systematically)
New Zealand	No (although some centres offer this)	No	Yes
Norway	Yes (not systematically)	Yes (health care)	Yes
Poland	No	No	No
Portugal	Yes	Yes (hospitality, retail, beauty care, construction, civil engineering)	/
Slovak Republic	/	/	/
Slovenia	No	No	No
Spain	Yes	?	Yes
Sweden	Yes (not systematically)	Yes (medical, architecture, engineering, and others)	Yes (not systematically)

	Vocational (General Workplace) Language Courses Available	Vocational Language Courses Targeting Specific Job Categories	On-the-Job Language Courses Available
Switzerland	Yes	Yes (construction, restaurant, cleaning, agriculture)	Yes
Turkey	No	No	Yes
United Kingdom	No	No	No
United States	Yes (not systematically)	/	Yes (not systematically)

Note: n.a. = information not available; See Table 1.1.
Source: OECD questionnaire on language training for adult migrants 2017.

7. Start by assessing learners' level of education, skills and capacity to learn and design courses accordingly

WHAT and WHY?

Adult migrants have very diverse educational backgrounds and literacy levels, and their needs in language training vary accordingly. In addition, each migrant has distinct personal circumstances, objectives and career prospects. This heterogeneity translates into diverse needs with respect to language training, practice, and learning paths.

There is a need for recognition that, while migrants who are literate in their own or another language can be seen as having skills to transfer to literacy in the new language, migrants with no literacy in their mother tongue require tutors with specific skills, knowledge, and competences and are better served in separate provision. As highlighted in Lesson 5, there is no 'one-size-fits-all' language trajectory, since reaching the same level of language proficiency is neither necessary nor feasible for people with different language repertoires, educational backgrounds, and career prospects (Beacco et al., 2014; Isphording, 2013; Chiswick and Miller, 2014).

While resource constraints may lead to learners of different skill-sets being taught together, the pace of progress will tend to differ along those skill levels. The course drop-out rate may be higher for those and the end of the skills scale (Cooke and Simpson, 2008). Ability grouping, meaning the placement of students in homogenised courses according to their ability or achievement level, enables adult learners to progress at an ideal pace and permits teachers to apply the most effective teaching methods for a given group of learners. To ensure that each migrant is referred to the language programme that best corresponds to their level of education and individual needs, countries need first to assess migrants' language competencies and proficiency needs and draw up an individualised learning plan, including together with the migrant.

WHO?

An initial assessment of host-country language proficiency and likelihood to quickly learn the language should be routinely undertaken for all new arrivals who are expected to remain in the country, independent of their immigration and employment status and origin. The use of separate tracks is particularly important for the illiterate, the low educated, the tertiary educated, and for speakers not familiar with the Latin alphabet. There is also an argument for organisation of monolingual speakers into groups based on broad language families (Arabic, Indo-Iranian, Romance, Slavic, etc.). Illiterate adults need to focus on oral basic language skills before learning how to study, read, and write. Low-educated learners, who are far away from the labour market, such as inactive mothers and the elderly, may gain a greater motivation to study when the course is focused on their specific real-world language needs. More generally, low-educated learners benefit from combined basic language learning and adult education, which represents a long-term investment with long-term payoffs, including for the children of learners. At the other end of the scale, highly skilled migrants require a faster-paced, more challenging learning atmosphere to attain the advanced linguistic resources required for skilled employment.

HOW?

Tools to assess learners' language level and needs can take various formats. All too often, for individuals without prior knowledge of the host-country language, prior education is used as a proxy for likely learning progress while other factors – including motivation – are often left aside in the assessment. To evaluate existing language skills, standardised language tests are the most prevalent form. However, other formats (such as survey questionnaires, samples of spoken and written production, and observations of language usage in migrants' professional activities) may be better suited to obtain an idea of the use learners will make of the language and to determine what types of content should be taught on a priority basis. Ideally, certified language experts meet with prospective learners on a one-on-one basis to find out about learning objectives and motivation, skills in other languages, education level, professional background, and language needs in migrants' daily life. Finland's largest contracted assessment provider, Testipiste, recognising that multiple cognitive factors are related to capacity for language acquisition (and that very few migrants will have any past exposure to Finnish), also evaluates structural perception and mathematics. Interviews of this kind can be complementary to a prior test and might, depending on migrants' level of proficiency, may be conducted in their native language.[9] This may require some upfront investment, but it shows migrants that educators understand and want to address their needs and interests, which, in turn, increases migrants' motivation to participate and succeed in training (see Lesson 2).

Once prospective learners' language abilities and objectives are assessed, countries can consider the following methods for course placement:

- Individual language learning plan
- Standard course grouping by level for prescribed number of hours
- Separate learning tracks based on educational background and literacy

Ideally, an individual language learning 'trajectory' –or tailor-made learning plan – should be developed in co-operation with each migrant. Based on learners' schedules and experiences, language experts identify the most appropriate learning option in the area and estimate the adequate number of hours of instruction and learning speed, given the structure of the course and the migrant's educational background and language repertoire. Reference and benchmarking tools like the Common European Framework of Reference for Languages (CEFR) and the Canadian Language Benchmarks/Niveaux de compétence linguistique canadiens help with this task. This first step allows learners to set realistic expectations and prevents 'course blocking' – which occurs when low-educated adult learners cannot progress onto a higher level, despite regular course attendance and high levels of motivation. Australia's Adult Migrant English Programme (AMEP), for example, uses individual pathway guidance at the start and end of each programme to maximise learners' outcomes. New learners receive an Individual Pathway Guide (IPG) that documents their learning goals and explains their rights and responsibilities as learners. The IPG also facilitates the monitoring of learners' outcomes during the programme. Once migrants have concluded the programme, they are interviewed about further learning needs and provided with a clearly delineated pathway to further language training, job search support, and education or vocational training opportunities.

Even with ability grouping, it is not possible to link a certain level of proficiency precisely to a certain number of hours of instruction. The efficiency of language training depends on the quality of training, the educational background of learners, and their opportunities to speak the host-country language outside of the classroom (Ramboll, 2007a). Across the OECD, language programmes diverge significantly in terms of the number of hours of instruction provided and the level of proficiency targeted, ranging from around 100 to 2 700 hours and from CEFR level A1 (i.e. basic everyday expressions) to level B1/B2 (i.e. interaction in most everyday situations). A few countries go beyond these levels. The most common level of support targets A2/B1. However, even within each level of the CEFR, migrants will have different skills and learning speeds. The number of hours provided to reach the target level may be insufficient for slow learners. At the same time, the target level may be too low for the labour market integration of high-skilled immigrants. Several OECD countries have therefore reformed language and integration courses, developing specific pathways and more flexible programmes for different types of learners and allowing migrants to repeat or skip levels as necessary. Such reforms do not automatically come at a higher cost, as there is often some overlap between different language offers and also because better targeting allows for faster individual progress. Finland, for example, efficiently reallocated existing resources to ensure a more differentiated, better targeted provision (Sarvimäki and Hämäläinen, 2012). Following an evaluation of its integration course system in 2007, Germany further extended its offering, introducing publicly funded specialised schemes with catch-up and intensive courses, and additional specific pathways for young adults, parents, and women. As a result of this evaluation, Germany also added the possibility to attend 300 additional lesson-hours if participants were not able to reach CEFR level B1. Another assessment of the scheme found significant improvements in terms of language skills, employment, and other integration outcomes linked to more differentiated training (Schuller et al., 2011). A modular system, as currently operates in Sweden and Denmark, which organises learning in consecutive modules with increasingly advanced learning goals, is another example of how countries can manage to provide high-quality, personalised language courses to a broad and diverse group of learners (see Box 7.2). This approach also allows for provision of additional modules for those migrants who seek to continue beyond the integration targets to reach their personal or professional objectives

---

Box 7.2. The Danish experience with modular language courses

Denmark provides language training to immigrants on a pre-paid deposit system. Courses are separated in three tracks, based on learners' educational background: Danish 1 for the illiterate and users of non-Latin alphabets, Danish 2 for the low-educated, and Danish 3 for multilingual speakers with higher education (minimum 12 years). Learners in Danish 1 (approx. 15% of learners in 2019) can use these hours to attain CEFR level A1 (mostly oral) and A2 (written) to pursue low-skilled work and achieve greater participation in social life. Danish 2 (approx. 43%) aims for level B1-B2 (oral/reading) and B1 (written), which qualifies learners for skilled work, further secondary or vocational education, and naturalisation requirements. Danish 3 (approx. 42%) leads to the 'Danish Language Proficiency Test' (level C1) that is necessary to access higher education in Denmark. Each track is sub-divided into six modules with tests at the end of each and a final exam at the end of the programme. Successful learners have the option to progress from Danish 1 to Danish 2 or 3. At the completion of each level, the deposit can be forwarded to cover costs for a new module.

Across the OECD, most state-sponsored language programmes have a separate 'literacy' track, involving 'pre-courses' in literacy and/or additional hours of instruction. Germany, for example, has two separate tracks, one for migrants who are literate in non-Latin writing systems and another for those with no literacy in any writing system. Still, concerns have been raised that there are insufficient options for transitioning these migrants to regular language courses after the alphabetisation course is completed (Wienberg, 2019). Tracking by education level is slightly less common, although pre-courses or additional hours are sometimes also extended to low-educated learners. Tracks for the tertiary educated are more ad hoc (e.g. for international students or workers in certain professions) and mostly available at an advanced level upon completion of a generic language course. Tracking by language repertoire is even more ad hoc and usually organised for one or two of the most common immigrant languages, while courses organised for broad language families are rare. Overall, even where such tracking exists, the availability of specialised tracking is often uneven across the country and concentrated in urban and immigrant-dense areas. Particularly in countries where migrants are spread over wide geographies, this may present a continued challenge. However, countries should consider how to use tracking more systematically to improve outcomes.

Table 7.1. Availability of Differentiated Learning Tracks in OECD countries, 2020 or latest available year

	Yes/No	If yes: Type of differentiation available
Australia	Yes	Migrants in the Adult Migrant English Program can choose pre-employment streams or social streams.
Austria	Yes	Literacy courses available, language courses are modular based on education level
Belgium	Yes	Literacy courses available
Canada	Yes	Settlement Program offers services at literacy, basic, and intermediate levels, as well as some employment-related language training
Chile	/	/
Colombia	/	/
Czech Republic	No	/
Denmark	Yes	Danish 1, 2, and 3 tracks target different levels of language learners (see Box 7.2)
Estonia	No	/
Finland	Yes	Four tracks, including one for literacy and one fast-track for integration of migrants assessed to have high learning capacity
France	Yes	Literacy courses are available, 3 pathways based on assessed French language ability (50, 100, or 200 hours)

	Yes/No	If yes: Type of differentiation available
Germany	Yes	Literacy courses are available. Intensive classes for highly educated learners are also possible.
Greece	No	/
Hungary	No	/
Iceland	/	/
Ireland	Yes	ESOL Literacy offering
Israel	/	/
Italy	No	/
Japan	No	/
Korea	No	/
Latvia	/	/
Lithuania	No	/
Luxembourg	Yes	Basic skills for beginners in French or German
Mexico	No	/
Netherlands	Yes	/
New Zealand	Yes	From Intensive Literacy and Numeracy to ESOL Level 3 for highly educated learners
Norway	Yes	/
Poland	No	/
Portugal	Yes	Literacy courses available through Adult Education and Training. Elementary course (target A2) has 6 modules, but 5 additional 'independent learner' modules are offered to reach B1
Slovak Republic	/	/
Slovenia	Yes	Slovene for Literacy (programme for adult migrants) is in development
Spain	Yes	Literacy courses available
Sweden	Yes	Three tracks based on educational background, each containing course levels A-D
Switzerland	Yes	All cantons have obligation to assess the individual migrant and offer modular courses, literacy courses available
Turkey	Yes	TÖMER (Turkish Learning Centres) provide language education for individuals seeking higher education.
United Kingdom	No	/
United States	No	Not systematically provided, although may be available

Note: n.a. = information not available; See Table 1.1.
Source: OECD questionnaire on language training for adult migrants 2017.

8. Engage with education specialists and non-traditional partners to design courses and broaden learning opportunities

WHAT and WHY?

Like language itself, second-language education is frequently evolving, and countries should be prepared to harness innovations to improve outcomes for migrants. By expanding the number of players involved in providing language experiences, governments can expand opportunities for individual migrants to acquire the linguistic tools required to fully participate in the host country's economy and society – along with possible additional benefits for broader socio-economic integration, by more closely linking migrants with the host-country society. What is more, by engaging with innovators in the field of education, either in the academic or private sector, policy makers can harness their experience not only to design programmes that have the best learning outcomes for migrants, but also potentially to provide services more efficiently at a lower cost. Non-profit organisations are also uniquely positioned to experiment, and have in particular shown a willingness to increase migrants' exposure to language through cultural exchange, often benefiting from a robust network of volunteers. Social engagement can both make language more meaningful and increase motivation while also giving migrants the opportunity to practise speaking in an immersive and low-stakes environment.

WHO?

Embracing new approaches requires engaging with new actors, namely, those who have been involved in their design, testing and development. Successful programmes are those that involve educators and scholars on language acquisition in the design process. New private-, public-, and social-sector partners may bring not only innovation and interdisciplinary expertise, but also cost savings to governments. Increasingly, countries have recognised that a multisectoral, "whole of society" approach that involves non-traditional stakeholders can simultaneously boost language and civic integration.

HOW?

Understanding which teaching tools and technologies have the best education outcomes is one way to help policy makers understand which tools will have the best labour market outcomes. Countries can benefit from the experience of partners such as:

- Educational institutions and second-language specialists

- Private sector actors
- Non-governmental organisations, social partners, and volunteer networks

Substantial work has been conducted in educational institutions that can provide instruction on effective course design. For example, many countries have embraced the lesson of differentiation in the classroom, specifically providing students with the same materials but explaining them in different ways and allowing students to manipulate those materials according to their levels (Tomlinson and Imbeau, 2010). Education specialists have determined that this is more sustainable in smaller classes, and in response, countries such as France have introduced a specific focus on creating smaller classes in their asylum or integration laws (OECD, 2019). When this is impossible, agencies can help teachers by creating more finely differentiated classes, through ability grouping (see Lesson 7). Another way to improve outcomes as class sizes increase is to provide one-on-one mentorship. Drawing from these lessons, countries such as Australia and Sweden as well as municipalities, such as Wroclaw in Poland,[10] have pursued peer matching or volunteer tutor programmes. To be effective, countries should consider the best way to recruit and retain

---

Box 8.1. Community College Brings Educational Research Base to its Partnership with Resettlement Agencies in the United States

Arizona's Refugee Resettlement Program uses Office of Refugee Resettlement Refugee Support Services funding to support the Refugee Education Program (REP) at Pima Community College (PCC) in Tucson, Pima County, Arizona. Prior to reductions in the United States refugee cap beginning in 2017, Pima County received over 1 000 officially designated refugees each year. Those in need of English language and literacy skills are referred to REP by local resettlement agencies. In 2017, REP served 790 migrant students.

All REP instructors are part of a professional learning community and are continuously trained in a number of innovative pedagogical methods. REP also works with the University of Arizona to train volunteers working with students with limited literacy.

REP instructors have developed a research-based placement assessment tool for adult emergent readers. Pre-testing happens at intake and registration, and post-testing happens at the end of each ten-week session. The teaching methodology is designed to build upon students' lived experiences and lead to higher-order-thinking skills in English and successful navigation of United State's systems. Methods include phonemic awareness and phonics, which are taught concurrently using the Language Experience Approach (connecting students' oral abilities to print by transcribing them). They also include Total Physical Response (using physical movement to react to or describe verbal input). A Whole-Part-Whole (meaning and context- linguistic parts- return to meaning and context) approach contextualises phonics in meaningful text while still allowing instructors to explore sound-symbol correspondences with their students.

Given a growing number of students who have lived in the United States for more than a year, REP has built new curricula balancing English for New Americans and College and Career Readiness English classes. Because the goal of federal resettlement services is to prepare migrants for employment as soon as possible, a specialised Vocational English Language Training curricula supports industries such as hospitality and manufacturing. REP meets with employers to maintain a current employment-focused curriculum.

PCC provides REP with in-kind services such as building space, facilities maintenance, use of IT and classroom equipment, IT services, books and materials. REP also opened a computer lab where students can receive drop-in help. Standard course activities make use of online and digital literacy resources.

---

volunteers across regions and programmes, perhaps through a centralised information management system. In the United States, academic partners and adult education researchers, frequently at the community college level, are often engaged directly in provision of language education to migrants (Box 8.1). In France, the Ministry of Interior has, in the context of the "Open the School to Parents for the Success of Children" (OEPRE) programme, expanded its partnership with the Ministry of National Education to better prepare language teachers and develop pedagogical resources. The aim is to further co-ordinate the OEPRE programme with the national integration plan and to further communication between pedagogical co-ordinators at the French Office for Immigration and Integration (OFII) and education experts.

Box 8.2. Private Sector Partners Engage in Experimentation in Finland

An innovative tool being explored by Finland is the Social Impact Bond, designed to catalyse private and institutional actors to customise integration services, including language training according to what is needed at the workplace. The EUR 14.2 million fund, piloted in 2016 as Koto-SIB Employment Programme and managed by Epiqus Oy, under the auspices of the Ministry of Economic Affairs and Employment, focuses on mobilising private expertise to move migrants quickly into the labour market. Outcome thresholds and metrics were designed collaboratively. The programme is focused on individual coaching and job matching.

While this programme is intended as a fast-track employment programme, for many of the career paths offered, the Finnish language is an essential component. Beginner, A2, and B1 Finnish groups are offered for the three- to four-month course. Unlike integration training, language teaching deploys a combination of different learning methods based on functional language comprehension and cognitive learning perception. Language courses are vocationally oriented, differentiation is carried out in-class, and internships begin when the migrant is deemed to have attained the requisite level of Finnish. The public sector only pays for the courses if participating migrants find employment.

There are some limitations. Migrants are only eligible for the programme if they can read and write in the Latin alphabet, for example. Only residents who are registered unemployed jobseekers can participate. The 2016 and 2017 cohorts were initially limited to immigrants in need of international protection. Data for the first fully inclusive cohort will not be available until late 2021, meaning a quantitative impact assessment is not expected until at the end of 2022. Still, interim results for August 2019 showed that by that time, 750 migrants from the initial focus group of 2 000 had found employment, at an estimated savings of EUR 20 million for the government. Employment outcomes were significantly higher for those in the training versus the control group.

The European Investment Bank produced a video to describe the programme and its successes: https://www.youtube.com/watch?v=9p8P_gimqpl.

In addition to academic partners, many OECD countries, such as Belgium, Denmark, Estonia, the Netherlands, and Switzerland, benefit from mobilisation of private sector actors in adult language learning, approving specific course providers as partners in their integration programmes or offering vouchers for migrants to use to pay for a course of their choosing. Denmark has designed financial incentives to encourage service providers to contribute to more efficient and individually oriented tuition (see Lesson 4; Ramboll, 2007b). Fewer countries have fully leveraged the private sector's capacity for agility and experimentation to design innovative integration programmes, but given the rapidly evolving technology sector and tight government budgets, such partnerships may yield important results. For example, with subsidies from the French Ministry of Culture (DGLFLF), the French language provider, CAVILAM – Alliance Française, developed the application "Français premiers pas," which is freely available and designed to help refugees and asylum seekers by providing the basics of the French language in a simple, accessible way. CAVILAM, which offers immersion courses at its technologically equipped facility in Vichy, has also positioned itself as a research centre and has developed courses for teachers of French, particularly focused on effective use of online teaching pedagogies. Finland has recently undertaken a pilot project on integration and language-training through social impact bonds (Box 8.2), where the government pays only when the private sector actor meets employment targets and efficiencies are gained. The programme is designed to provide migrants with the tools they require to move into the labour market as quickly as possible and aims to provide language instruction in a hands-on way.

Box 8.3. Supporting the Development of Theatrical Practices for Language Learning in Portugal

With their ability to experiment, foundations and non-profit organisations can serve as centres for innovation. They can also support and expand programmes that arise organically in response to a perceived need. In Portugal, language teachers of the Portuguese Refugee Council (CPR) founded the amateur theatre group, RefugiActo, in 2004, having identified the need for a forum to allow refugee voices to be heard. The group developed theatrical productions to raise awareness of the need for social inclusion in Portuguese society, but it also noted the potential for improved integration outcomes for migrants. From February 2014 to January 2017, CPR partnered with the PARTIS – Artistic Practices for Social Inclusion – initiative of the Calouste Gulbenkian Foundation in Lisbon to promote theatre and dramatic bodily expression as strategies facilitating language acquisition of asylum seekers and refugees. Through the project, "Refuge and Theatre: A Thousand Gestures Sleep in My Fingers," the theatre programme benefited from support designed to ground the project and ensure its durability, as well as from external evaluation of its methodologies. Financial support enabled the non-profit to dedicate staff full-time to development of innovative techniques. Having begun the project at a time when migrant flows to Portugal were relatively low and service provision was decentralised, the CPR/PARTIS programme was well-situated to respond to increased demand and interest from 2015 onward.

One aim of the project was to create a document that could be widely disseminated to groups interested in using theatrical techniques to improve language learning, not only for refugees, but for all migrants in need of social inclusion. The document, a "Notebook of Theatrical Practices for the Learning of the Language" has been published in Portuguese and English. It provides a toolkit for following the methodology of "learning by doing," mimicry, and improvisation to relieve the stress caused by the real-life situations, such as medical appointments and relations with immigration services, that inspire the lessons (Galvão and Cabrita, 2020). An artist and a teacher of Portuguese as a Foreign language designed the exercises with close attention to the themes of A1/A2 language learning levels.

Finally, it is important to acknowledge that language learning can be enriched by increased exposure to social life in the host language. Integration activities and language learning can be seen as mutually reinforcing. Most OECD countries rely on non-profit organisations that provide conversation groups and "language buddy" mentoring (see Špačková and Štefková, 2006). In Ireland, the Third Age Foundation runs the Fáilte Isteach project, which supports weekly conversation groups involving 1 200 elderly Irish volunteers and 3 200 immigrant learners through 104 branches across the country. In Luxembourg, the Café des Langues promotes language tables and the opportunity to enjoy food with new friends. An artist platform and start-up incubator in Paris, France, the 104,[11] provided language learning activities for recently arrived migrants through theatre classes, allowing the interaction and cultural exchange between migrants and long-standing artists (see Box 8.3 for a similar example from Portugal). In several countries, including Denmark, Finland, France, Germany, Ireland Italy, and the Netherlands, language buddies have organised exchanges around sport, and in 2016, a European Commission report outlined good practices in designing such programmes for social inclusion (European Commission, 2016). Non-profit organisations may also fill a co-ordination function in countries with decentralised programmes. The International Rescue Committee (IRC) in the United States has, for example, developed an online information hub called Switchboard that, in addition to connecting migrants with local resources, offers a library of learning resources and e-courses.[12]

Some countries have also expressly incorporated community engagement into integration programmes, recognising that non-traditional stakeholders are well positioned to offer language immersion and cultural learning, but that they require resources and co-ordination to remain viable. Canada's Settlement Program includes services that focus on building connections and promoting social cohesion. A wide variety of activities support informal language learning for newcomers, such as conversation circles, peer support through recreation activities, community events, and matching opportunities for cross-cultural exchange with Indigenous peoples and broader host communities. Australia has recently prioritised extension of interaction with faith communities. The Portuguese High Commission for Migration expressly promotes Non-formal Educational Actions in recognition of the fact that diverse learners require diverse learning opportunities. In Latvia, the Ministry of Culture has funded an improvisational theatre language club. Several countries have introduced a model of integration activities in which mothers can participate alongside their children, including Austria, Estonia, Germany, Iceland, and Italy. Immigration New Zealand supports the "Welcoming Communities" programme, which – while not expressly dedicated to language learning – brings migrants together with native-born members of their local communities to build connections for better social and economic participation. Similar initiatives exist in Australia, Canada, and the United States. Such programmes have the added benefit of potentially reducing the number of course hours needed for civic integration programmes by indirectly encouraging social inclusion in the host community.[13] Direct Government involvement also reduces the potential for dilution of responsibility that that may occur with the addition of multiple stakeholders.

9. Ensure efficient co-ordination between stakeholders to avoid overlap and under-coverage and guarantee common standards across the country

WHAT and WHY?

While many stakeholders are involved in language training, there is often little to no co-ordination between them, which may lead to overlap in certain areas and under-coverage in others. Often, different integration and employment actors fund, independently advertise, and develop their own criteria for their own courses. The result is such that – even where appropriate courses exist – potential learners may not be informed or eligible. Wide variation also exists regarding the degree of centralised control over curricula, teacher qualifications, course-provider accreditation, testing mechanisms, and the extent to which government funding is conditional upon certain measures of quality assurance. Indeed, most programmes are at least partially funded at the national level, but implemented – and sometimes even designed – at the regional or local level. To avoid overlap and gaps in language training, and to ensure common standards across the country, transparent and regular co-ordination will be required between the national and local level and between different local stakeholders.

WHO?

Whereas regular language training is often funded by municipalities or agencies under the auspices of the Ministry of Interior, training that is geared to the labour market is commonly financed by the public employment service (Table 9.1). Vocational training is frequently offered by a diffuse set of actors and funded by stakeholders with different objectives. These providers may lack accredited language teachers and use curricula that are detached from those of standard language courses. Language training providers, in turn, regularly lack expertise in relevant job sectors (Pöyhönen, and Tarnanen, 2015).

HOW?

Management of this multi-level and multi-stakeholder process can take several forms:

- When local authorities play a stronger role in the development and provision of services, some co-ordination mechanism may be required
- A centralised agency or ministry can take responsibility for co-ordination of actors
- The central government can take responsibility for standard-setting

An increasing number of OECD countries have decentralised integration, including language training, giving local governments and civil society increased responsibility. This may be one way to improve local migrant integration, as decisions are made in the communities where the migrants live. Several OECD countries have increased the management role of municipalities in recent years. In some countries, such as Denmark and the United States, such an arrangement is longstanding. In Poland and Spain, civil society also plays an important role. In late 2019, the Polish Foundation "Okno na Wschód" created a Centre for Supporting Foreigners, which, in addition to organising Polish language courses, also provides broader integration advice. In some countries, notably Germany and Italy, centres for adult education are active in provision of language courses. The Italian Ministry of Education funds more than 500 Provincial Adult Education Centres that have long been host to basic literacy and Italian courses. Since integration legislation in 2009 imposed a language requirement, the Ministry of Interior, which organises the language tests, has also provided support to these centres. Whatever the division of responsibility, authorities, service-providers, and experts should meet regularly to inform each other about existing course formats, discuss possible synergies, and pool together all available financial and human resources to develop a more diverse, adaptable and transparent offer.

The growing importance of local actors has placed emphasis on the growing need for co-ordination to guarantee availability and consistent provision of language learning options across the country. Without such co-ordination and communication, it is much more difficult for countries with decentralised programmes to assess whether demand is met, to collect data on outcomes, or to adapt to changing circumstances. For example, a report by the Norwegian Research Institute, Fafo, on adaptation of introduction activities – chief among which is language learning – during the novel coronavirus (COVID-19) pandemic showed that one in two municipalities faced difficulties in adapting to the new situation (Fafo, 2020). A lack of co-ordination may also delay the mainstreaming of innovations developed in specific municipalities – often large cities – resulting in unequal opportunities for more remote regions.

Ideally, one single actor handles the enrolment of learners and their orientation to available course-providers. This 'one-stop-shop' function allows for greater visibility of the programme, more common quality standards for enrolment, and more informed choices by learners in selection of course-providers. Those overseeing the provision of training should then be responsible for setting common standards and ensuring that these standards are consistently applied by all providers throughout the national territory. Countries that have recently shifted responsibilities to improve efficient delivery of programmes include Australia (Commonwealth Co-ordinator-General for Migrant Services) and Finland (Ministry of Economic Affairs and Employment).

In most OECD countries, standard-setting and quality control is performed by government agencies or non-governmental agents entrusted by the government at the national level (Rossner, 2014a and 2014b; see Box 9.1 for examples of experience of co-ordinating stakeholders in language training). Quality control should be carried out by specialists for adult education and may take the form of unexpected checks of a sample of classes or interviews with randomly selected participants about specific aspects of their training. The frequency of such inspections should balance considerations of the need for quality oversight with administrative burden and the anticipated likelihood of material change. In some countries, quality control involves accreditation under a mandatory scheme, which usually includes a more formal periodic inspection. France, for example, has accredited language course providers since 2011 through the 'French as Language of Integration' (FLI) label, which entails an audit and an inter-ministerial commission opinion once every three years. The United Kingdom inspects and evaluates ESOL courses and tests through two independent agencies – the Office for Standards in Education (OFSTED) and the Office of Qualifications and Examinations Regulation (OFQUAL). Another way to ensure efficient allocation of public resources and to support the maintenance of high-quality training across regions and providers is to introduce results-based financing and benchmarking for language providers, as is currently practised in the Netherlands and Denmark (Gortz et al., 2006; Ramboll, 2007b; Significant, 2010). Greater co-operation and a more efficient allocation of resources can also have a direct impact on language and employment outcomes, as was recently observed in Finland (Sarvimäki and Hämäläinen, 2012) and Italy (OECD, 2014). In recognition of this, some OECD countries, such as Ireland, Estonia, and Lithuania, have made greater co-ordination and a "whole of government response" part of their recent action plans on migrant integration (see Box 9.1).

Box 9.1. Experience with co-ordination of stakeholders in charge of language training

The co-ordination of language training in Germany was significantly enhanced by the implementation of the 2005 Immigration Law, which merged and standardised the various previously existing programmes into a more consistent offer of integration courses. Integration Courses are developed by the Federal Office for Migration and Refugees. The Goethe Institute – Germany's worldwide cultural and language institute – created the essential basic course content, teacher qualification concept, and the 'German Test for Immigrants' (DTZ), which was developed in co-operation with the test provider, telc gGmbH. For vocational language courses, telc gGmbH has created an extensive catalogue of learning objectives, the final exam, and the teacher qualification concept since 2016. Funding is federal but courses are implemented locally by a wide range of accredited institutions, which must employ qualified German teachers (trained pre-or-in-service), follow a framework curriculum, and use a standardised final exam.

In Austria, several federal agencies are involved – in co-ordination with the Bundesländer – in the integration of migrants. Additionally, civil society is often charged with implementation by regional authorities. The general responsibility for migrant integration lies with the Integration Agency under the Federal Chancellery (BKA), and other courses are run through the Public Employment Service (AMS). To avoid fragmentation and horizontal differentiation, the Austrian Government launched its National Action Plan for Integration in 2010 and followed up with 50 Action Points in 2016. The Strategy for Promotion of Language (Sprachförderstrategie) aims to create a common structure and didactic approach for various models of welcome classes, to delineate responsibilities for certain language levels and categories of migrants to specific stakeholders (BMI, BKA, AMS), and to create a common funding strategy on the part of large granters, both state and federal (Integration Report, 2016).

Each canton in Switzerland has authority to establish course eligibility and to set the number of hours and types of courses offered. However, cantons are guided by goals established under the Cantonal Integration Programmes, launched in 2014, and they receive some central government funding. Additionally, the national programme, "fide", in conjunction with the State Secretariat for Migration, aims to homogenise the quality of language courses, teaching methods, and examinations. It provides a tool to assign migrants to different courses according to their needs and ability. If a course is evaluated and found not to meet these standards, the service provider loses the fide certification (www.fide-info.ch).

Ireland launched a co-ordinated "whole of government response" to integration for 2017-20, an important pillar of which was the facilitation of English to Speakers of Other Languages (ESOL). Among the priorities of the Migrant Integration Strategy were the certification of course participants' achievements and establishment of a formal progression which could be benchmarked against the Common European Framework of Reference for Languages. The Minister of State at the Department of Justice and Equality with responsibility for Equality, Immigration and Integration was tasked with creation of a Strategy Committee to oversee implementation (Migrant Integration Strategy, 2016).

Table 9.1. Actors involved in financing for publicly financed language programmes in OECD countries, 2020 or latest available year

	Actors involved in financing of language training in OECD countries
Australia	Department of Home Affairs; Adult Migrant English Program (AMEP)

	Actors involved in financing of language training in OECD countries
Austria	Federal Chancellery, Ministry of Labour, Austrian Integration Fund; regional governments and PES
Belgium	Public Planning Service – Social Integration; Flemish Interior Ministry; Agency for Civil Integration (Flanders); Community Commission (Brussels); Ministre de l'Action sociale et le Service public de Wallonie Intérieur et Action (Wallonia); The German-Speaking Community
Canada	Immigration, Refugees, and Citizenship Canada (IRCC); 10 provinces and 3 territories
Chile	/
Colombia	/
Czech Republic	Ministry of Labour and Social Affairs; Ministry of Interior; 18 Integration Centres; Ministry of Education, Youth and Sports
Denmarkⁱ	Ministry of Immigration and Integration; Ministry of Finance; municipalities
Estonia	Ministry of the Interior; Ministry of Education and Research; the Ministry of Culture; the Ministry of Social Affairs; the and the Ministry of Justice
Finland	Ministry of Economic Affairs and Employment (allocates funding to regional Centres for Economic Development, Transport and the Environment); Ministry of Education and Culture
France	Ministry of the Interior, La Direction générale des étrangers en France (DGEF)
Germany	Federal Office for Migration and Refugees (BAMF); Ministry of Labour; Ministry of Interior
Greece	Ministry of Economy, Development, and Tourism; Ministry of Education; Ministry of Migration and Asylum
Hungary	Ministry of Interior
Iceland	/
Ireland	Office for the Promotion of Migrant Integration; Funds Administration Unit of the Department of Justice and Equality; Department of Education and Skills; Department of Social Protection
Israel	Ministry of Aliyah and Integration; Ministry of Education; Jewish Agency
Italy	Ministry of the Interior, Department for Civil Liberties and Immigration; Ministry of Education; provincial and municipal governments
Japan	Ministry of Health, Labour, and Welfare (regarding "Training Course for Promoting Stable Employment of Foreign Residents")
Korea	Ministry of Justice
Latvia	Ministry of the Interior; Ministry of Culture
Lithuania	European Social Fund Agency under the Ministry of Social Security and Labour
Luxembourg	Ministry of Education; National Language Institute (INL); National Reception Office
Mexico	Mexican Commission of Aid to Refugees; Sin Fronteras (non-profit organisation)
Netherlands	Ministry of Social Affairs and Employment (Uitvoering van beleid SZW); municipal governments
New Zealand	Department of Education, Tertiary Education Commission, regional governments
Norway	Ministry of Education; Norwegian Directorate for Education and Training; Skills Norway; municipal governments
Poland	Ministry of the Interior, Department of European Funds; municipal governments
Portugal	High Commission for Migration; Ministry of Solidarity, Employment and Social Security; Ministry of Education and Science
Slovak Republic	Ministry of the Interior
Slovenia	Ministry of the Interior
Spain	Ministry of Education; Autonomous Communities; Ministry of Labour, Migration, and Social Security
Sweden	Ministry of Education; Ministry of Employment; municipalities
Switzerland	Central government, Cantons, and municipalities
Turkey	/
United Kingdom	Home Office; Department for Communities and Local Government
United States	Department of Education; Office of Refugee Resettlement (Department of Health and Human Services); state and local governments

Note: n.a. = information not available; / = not applicable; See Table 1.1.
ⁱ· Denmark is the only EU Member State that does not receive funds from the Asylum, Migration and Integration Fund (AMIF), due to the opt-out on EU Justice and Home Affairs. The Hungarian AMIF programme was partially suspended in 2018.
Source: OECD questionnaire on language training for adult migrants 2017.

10. Build on new technologies in language learning

WHAT and WHY?

The use of Information and Communications Technology (ICT) tools in education has enormous potential to expand the reach and cost-effectiveness of language learning for newcomers. E-learning tools can complement – though not replace – face-to-face-learning. Thoughtful application of Computer-Assisted Language Learning (CALL) can allow language teachers to engage in greater differentiation according to the needs of individual migrants. They can increase migrant motivation simply by making the courses more varied and interesting. Integrating new technology in the classroom may reduce student-teacher contact hours and costs related to teaching work when coupled with appropriate organisational change. Moreover, CALL and distance learning can lead to better outcomes for language-learners who relocate to remote areas where services are less readily available and can provide access to language training for pre-departure migrants. Knowledge about what works best and in which contexts will be a prerequisite for harnessing these tools. Once they are in place, platforms can facilitate data collection that can enhance monitoring of teacher efforts and student results, information that can be used to further improve innovation and quality (bearing in mind the need to safeguard individual privacy). At the same time, policy makers must be aware of the potential barriers to use of such tools to avoid pitfalls in implementation.

Furthermore, the recent experience of the novel coronavirus (COVID-19) pandemic has made evident the need for reliable distance learning in situations where in-person learning is impossible. Countries that had not developed distance learning found themselves faced with the need to identify partners and ramp up such programmes rapidly. The alternative was to halt language learning opportunities and postpone proficiency examinations. Others that had a distance tool available still noted that participation was not possible for every migrant. Countries could benefit from this experience by identifying areas for improvement so they may be better prepared for similar events in the future.

WHO?

Digital tools for language are already in place in a majority of OECD countries, although the scale and scope differ widely. Language providers or state agencies can build programmes in consultation with experts in the use of ICT in pedagogy. Teachers can integrate these tools into their teaching, reducing preparation time and enabling more efficient use of in-class hours with students. E-learning tools may be especially useful for migrants with higher education levels and can provide flexibility for active job seekers. Finally, it is essential to factor in the need to build applications that run smoothly and technical support to ensure that devices used in the classroom are operational.

HOW?

In the domain of ICT-based learning, there is no one-size-fits-all solution, but there are many combinations and tools from which to choose. While the use of technology and distance learning is relatively new for most countries tackling integration issues (as of 2010, only the Netherlands made systematic use of ICT in its integration exam and offered a standardised study package with ICT components [Kluzer, et al., 2011]), most OECD countries have made steps toward increasing the use of such programmes. ICT-based language provision for adult migrants has tended to grow in a bottom-up fashion, but co-ordinated government strategies and evaluations should improve consistency in service delivery and tie the tools more effectively to any eventual testing or integration objectives.

A first step is defining the quality criteria and standards that will be used to choose ICT-based learning resources. Understanding of which combination of tools and contexts can lead to the best outcomes is still emerging. The majority of data collected to date on the subject comes in the form of teacher and student questionnaires, and many countries are still experimenting (Box 10.1). Determining which combination of tools best meets the needs of a specific integration programme and under which context requires consideration of the features that can be uniquely afforded by digital learning environments and an examination of the boundary conditions under which instructional techniques are most effective. The socio-pedagogical research base can offer significant lessons – computers have been used for language-learning to various degrees in various countries since the 1960s – and educators can provide meaningful guidance to government bodies charged with designing or selecting tools. However, the best way to evaluate the pedagogical effectiveness of CALL is still being debated, and authorities must consider the needs of specific populations of migrants. For some, a fully online course may better suit their needs than an in-person course that incorporates ICT materials. Some migrants may be better suited to self-study, while others may benefit more from teacher-led programmes. Generally, OECD countries have approached ICT in three ways:

- Blended learning, in which ICT tools are integrated into the physical classroom
- Digital classrooms, fully online platforms for distance learning
- Digital tools, such as apps and videos, for independent study

Generally, it is recognised that the most successful use of technology in language study has been in partnership with in-person engagement with a teacher. This approach avoids loss of nuance and ensures adequate explanation of errors (Kluzer, et al., 2011).[14] Tools developed in Canada, Germany, Italy, Lithuania, and Spain have all prioritised blended learning. In this context, ICT is considered a complement to language tuition, rather than a substitute. It can enable diverse forms of learning (i.e. videos for visual learners or news reports and dialogues for auditory learners), allowing migrants to follow customised learning paths while still permitting group engagement in the classroom. Use of technology in a classroom environment also gives migrants access to richness of material and new techniques without requiring them to invest in their own devices or internet connection.

However, there may be room for ICT to substitute for certain aspects of traditional language education, most notably for the classroom itself. ICT learning provides flexibility, as it may allow migrants to learn at any time or location, including pre-departure. Australia, Austria, Finland, Israel, and Norway have developed virtual classrooms for distance learning. It is also possible to adapt the blended systems of both Spain and Germany to distance learning. Migrants in Australia have responded positively to the flexibility of the distance AMEP programme, pointing to the advantages of better managing childcare or work obligations. Others have noted the ease of access when living in a remote location. In Finland, distance learning has brought together the small number of migrants throughout the south-western region seeking to integrate in Swedish. Such programmes can also facilitate differentiation, as teachers can engage simultaneously with more than one student across disparate locations via private chat or assign tailored homework without demotivating students who progress at different speeds.

Box 10.1. Countries have made the effort to improve digital offerings

Estonia's e-courses (www.keeleklikk.ee) are funded by the Estonian Ministry of Education and Science and the European Social Fund. Courses are designed for both English and Russian speakers and are supported by an Estonian teacher with whom the learners can exchange messages via email. The Austrian ÖIF maintains a language portal, Mein Sprachportal, which provides an overview of different language courses offered. It includes access to a variety of video and audio tools that allow migrants to test their language skills and prepare for tests. Since 2017, The French Ministry of Interior has collected a variety of online tools, including several Massive Open Online Courses (MOOCs), in response to a call for projects launched by the Directorate of Reception, Support for Foreigners, and Nationality (DAAEN, since an 5 October 2020 reorganisation, now the Directorate of Integration and Access to Nationality (DIAN)).

Germany has developed similar tools, including a learning portal (vhs-Lernportal) that allows students to link with tutors who can view their progress. Different types of exercises are presented through various media: audio, video, pictures, and written text. The portal can be used for homework outside of in-person classes, as teachers can use color-coded markers to electronically correct student mistakes and track areas for further learning. It is also available for free self-study if learners so choose. The portal is both desktop and smartphone compatible.

Since 2010, Canada's LearnIT2teach project has supported blended learning through hosting of courseware and training teachers on how to adapt these tools for their learners. In 2020, IRCC launched an enhanced solution for language training providers, Avenue.ca, an internet-based system for the planning, delivery, and management of settlement language training. The website offers a virtual space for teachers to store and share resources, the Avenue Moodle platform, and attendance tracking for teachers to check how much time each learner spends working on their Moodle course.

The Sacramento County Office of Education – a centre of expertise in design and use of instructional technology in adult learning – provides "United States Learns", funded by the United States and Californian Departments of Education. The programme includes a free website and apps that can be used by ESL teachers or independently. Notable tools include games and the ability to record and playback the user's voice and compare it to proficient spoken English.

Portugal's Online Platform for Learning Portuguese, offered by the High Commission for Migration, allows learners to progress through two modules, beginner and independent. The course is designed to build vocabulary learning, listening, reading, and writing skills, as well as expanded grammar knowledge. Users are invited to register and identify a native language, in addition to providing data regarding education level, employment status, and knowledge of other languages. Instructions and materials, such as the online dictionary, are made available in that language. The lessons and the tools needed to complete them are explained through both text and audio. Each module contains progress tests to advance to new levels.

Digital tools for self-learning on computer, tablet, or smartphone have grown rapidly on the market. Many are nominally diversified to cater toward different learner profiles. Particularly for learning at the lowest levels, technologies that do not permit spoken interaction are often considered ineffective in building oral capabilities. However, although results are closely correlated to variation in user motivation, some app-based learning has succeeded in building vocabulary (Loewen et al., 2020). Apps can also be an effective way to provide instant feedback regarding errors. Digital tools can also provide time flexibility for homework assignments. Countries like Austria, Germany, Luxembourg, and local governments in the United Kingdom and the United States have invested in language learning applications. They are typically freely available online and present gamified modules in which learners can watch videos and respond to questions, tracking their progress.[15]

ICT-based language platforms offer a good solution for advanced or highly specialised courses, where the number of interested learners is often insufficient for classroom-based learning. Such platforms do not need to be fully integrated with a language programme. Highly educated learners can take advantage of self-study options. Stand-alone tools, including the German "Ein Tag in der Pflege" (One Day in the Hospital) app for nurses or New Zealand's WorkTalk website (see Box 10.2), can address specifically identified areas for improvement in language usage.

Box 10.2. New Zealand Provides Online Tools to Skilled Workers

WorkTalk was developed by Immigration New Zealand in collaboration with the Language in the Workplace Team of the School of Linguistics and Applied Language Studies, Te Herenga Waka – Victoria University of Wellington. The programme was designed in recognition of the fact that for some workers, particularly those with an already advanced language level, culturally specific language usage can be as important as grammar and vocabulary. In addition to providing practice workplace scenarios for migrants, the website also offers tips and tools for employers, as well as an interactive test through which users can judge their understanding of nuanced phrases and appropriate replies. Importantly, this tool, along with much of the New Zealand Now website, is available to offer advice and lessons to migrants pre-departure.

In addition to assessing where digital tools are likely to be most effective, governments must also consider financing. The cost to develop tools for CALL is considerable, and the reality is that integrating these tools may not reduce cost of language courses, at least not in the short term. The economics of on-line courses are complex, involving not only the cost of the tools, but also a change in approach to the management of teaching and finances. For instance, where governments develop their own tools, this requires up-front investment, development of business plans, project management, training and technical support to teachers, and a team approach to course development and delivery. Some governments, such as the Netherlands, have chosen instead to approve or license privately developed ICT platforms, which often charge a fee. Every case is different, and countries must develop a model based on their goals and requirements. If the tools can enrich the learning process and improve outcomes, they may offer significant returns vis-à-vis labour market integration.

While ICT is an area of high potential, policy makers must be aware of and actively seek solutions to the most common barriers to integration of CALL:

* Affordability of computer hardware and software and stable Internet connectivity;
* Technical and theoretical knowledge; and
* Acceptance of the technology by both student and teacher.

If CALL is integrated in a classroom setting, hardware must be maintained to avoid technical malfunctions disrupting course hours. Software programmes to be used outside of class should be designed to work easily on hardware that most migrants possess. Low-income families are more likely to have access to a smartphone than a desktop computer with internet access, for example, but they could be guaranteed access to desktops at public libraries or learning centres (Rideout and Katz, 2016).[16] It is important that migrants not be penalised for lack of technology by missing out on coursework. To overcome this challenge, some course providers supply migrants with the necessary devices, for example in Israel and Finland.

Box 10.3. Lessons in Distance Learning During Lockdown

To ensure continuity of integration during confinement, France provided 15-24 hours of distance learning per week to those migrants who had already begun French courses under their integration contract. Because of the need for internet access and basic technological and French literacy, distance training was targeted toward 100-hour courses (for migrants closest to A1 level during initial placement) with groups of 6-10 participants, and 200-hour courses with groups of 3-5 participants. Out-of-class work took place via app, digital learning wall (a visual classroom display designed to focus learning), and email. Individual support and follow-up on written exercises was provided. The programme was only introduced on a small scale to test the approach. Based on the lessons taken from the experiment, France plans to integrate e-learning modalities into their general course offerings in the future.

Germany, which had online options in place (see also Box 10.1) through its Volkshochschul-Verband (association of adult education centres), invested EUR 20 million and approved nearly 9 300 online classes to avoid disruption of courses due to suspension of government services during spring 2020 and winter 2020-21. Approximately 66 000 migrants (plus about 8 600 course repeaters) transitioned to the online classes, which were offered free of charge during this period. The Federal Office for Migration and Refugees found that many migrants enjoyed the online offerings during periods of confinement, but decided that because of limitations in enabling personal educational accompaniment and exchange amongst participants, online courses taken during the confinement period would be a "bonus" that would not count against the migrant's language learning entitlement. At the same time, Germany also increased efforts to support regular courses in their online transition, providing additional funding to education centres that could be spent on devices needed for online teaching.

During lockdown, Austria's Österreichischer Integrationsfonds provided free online language courses for levels A1-B1, and 75 000 eligible migrants participated. Approximately 70% of the participants were women. Given the project's popularity, the ministry is considering maintaining blended and online courses going forward. Additionally, in December 2020 – during the lockdown of the hospitality industry – Austria's Österreichischer Integrationsfonds, together with the Viennese Economic Chamber, began providing tailored online language courses for employees of the hospitality and catering industry.

A call for projects through Open Door in Sweden also resulted in several innovative solutions to migrant isolation. For example, the non-profit Kompis Sverige (Buddy Sweden) launched "Language Buddy Online," matching migrants with native Swedish speakers to increase interpersonal connections while advancing language practice. Estonia launched a similar programme, The Volunteer Language Friends project, advertised through social media, which linked volunteer mentors to language learners through e-channels. Volunteers were offered short trainings by Estonian Language House teachers from the Integration Foundation. In Finland, educational institutions continued to provide distance teaching, taking into account students' learning abilities and access to technology. An option to return homework assignments by mail was introduced.

The Swiss "COVID-19 Special Situation Ordinance" prohibited face-to-face courses beginning 2 November 2020, but an exception was made for courses up to Level A2 for those learners unable to participate in online education due to very low language level or lack of digital literacy or connectivity. Group sizes were limited to 15 people. Additional innovations, such as Cours de français au parc (French language teaching in the park) in Geneva, emerged as ways to maintain social engagement and language training for the vulnerable while adhering to safety protocols. At the same time, financing was adapted to allow cantons to use federal funding to acquire computer equipment that could be lent to learners studying remotely.

Especially if materials are meant to enable independent learning, tools should be kept simple. Instructions should assume low prior technical knowledge, and the interface should avoid unneeded, distracting material (Mayer, 2019). Some migrants will need time to build basic digital skills. Australia provides books and CDs for AMEP distance learners at the beginner level, then encourages a transition to online tools as the students progress (Social Compass, 2019).

Learners with no prior exposure to the host language would benefit from availability of materials in their native language, ideally in both written and oral forms. Several tools developed on the market in the Netherlands are designed to increase user-friendliness for illiterate and very early learners, for whom audio- and video-based resources like podcasts and slow-speed content can help improve listening skills without the barrier of written materials (Kluzer, et al., 2011).[17] To date, however, few governments have undertaken to translate materials into a variety of languages. Estonia's programme is available in Russian and English, and the Slovakia, with European Commission support, provides a free website in 13 languages to learn the Slovak, up to level B2.[18]

Adult language learners can be hesitant to trust online tools to the same degree as in-person language learning, but this can be overcome by better illustrating the opportunities associated with CALL. When successful tools are developed, they should be promoted, along with explanations of the flexibility and results they provide. Online tools must also be of proven quality. ICT integration is a fast-evolving sector. Because the options for CALL are growing, policy makers need a way to understand and evaluate the quality of the various offerings. For example, there must be a straightforward way to identify whether the information is up to date. Integration agencies should also include a comparison of outcomes using digital versus in-person tools in their impact evaluations (Hartikainen, et al., 2020).

During the COVID-19 confinement period, it became evident that there is currently little alternative to presence learning for the most vulnerable groups – especially migrants with low literacy skills. It is essential to understand how best to reach those migrants who are likely to encounter difficulties and to tackle those difficulties, because deferring classes altogether, even when examinations are also postponed, likely results in learning losses and potential dropouts. Many countries are still evaluating how to maximise retention rates when transitioning to fully distance learning. Those with longstanding and successful distance programmes, such as Finland, emphasise the desirability of a first in-person meeting to build trust, periodic check-ins, and the teacher's preparedness to engage the students.[19] For newer programmes, the impact of COVID-19-related confinements could provide an informative natural experiment. Germany noted that, while many learners responded positively to moving coursework online, some students also dropped from the programme. France reported good success with keeping students engaged, but its online courses were targeted to students who had already reached a certain level. An assessment of Australia's online courses suggested that the move online worked well for those with caring responsibilities, but not for humanitarian migrants or groups with low literacy. While 80% of all students said they improved their skills during the lockdown period, 70% stated that their skills would have improved more in a classroom setting. Given these lessons (see Box 10.3), an evaluation may be able to differentiate between groups of migrants who are more or less likely to succeed in an online course environment. For countries that have not yet developed a distance programme option, COVID-19 provides an opportunity to understand the consequences by comparing outcomes to those countries that had such tools in place.

11. Invest in teacher preparation and recruitment

WHAT and WHY?

Improving access to language training is not enough by itself. Course quality is equally important, both regarding retention and with respect to improving outcomes for adult migrants. In addition to mobilising the right tools, this requires well-qualified teachers. Student-teacher relationships can be essential to fostering motivation to continue in a language course. Teachers are also in the best position to differentiate according to the needs demonstrated by students in the classroom. They provide important feedback to learners and are capable of filling gaps, for example by explaining nuance in the meaning of words and expressions. Well-prepared teachers can make the difference for better language outcomes.

Language training in the adult migrant context is different from traditional foreign language education. Even within ability groups, teachers will encounter students with a wide range of backgrounds. Exposure outside the classroom to the host-country language will differ according to the socio-economic situation of the migrant, leading learning needs to vary significantly. Some migrants will, depending on their language contacts, need to dedicate more practice to speaking, listening, or reading. Others may be exposed to specific dialects in their social context and need to understand how those differ from standard language. Second, adult migrants have specific linguistic needs tied their status as migrants in a potentially unfamiliar country with its particular systems. In some cases, legal concerns regarding the status of residence or psychological effects of past trauma may add pressure to the learning situation. Such migrants may require more psychosocial support during their attendance in language courses to be successful (Krumm and Plutzar, 2008). Language teachers may be confronted with questions and problems resulting from these conditions that educators are not usually prepared to handle. Third, unlike with much traditional foreign language teaching, teachers of migrants are often addressing a multilingual audience. While some migrants may have little to no language learning experience, others may have two or even three family languages. Responding to these heterogeneous experiences in planning a curriculum is an essential part of the role of the teacher (Cooke and Simpson, 2008).

The integration of CALL into a classroom setting raises additional teacher preparation issues. New technologies entail new 'literacy' requirements, not only for language learners. Numerous qualitative case studies have revealed a negative attitude among teachers toward the use of ICT, which largely reflects insufficient experience in this domain. Their own ICT literacy and educational philosophy can be significant barriers for teachers to fully engage in use of new technologies,[20] which can mean a loss of investment for those countries who have invested in development of these tools.

The need to be qualified in these specific areas has, in some countries, led to a shortage of available educators. There is substantial competition for well-qualified teachers. Furthermore, private sector salaries may be more attractive. To ensure that eligible migrants have access to language courses needed to fulfil integration obligations or entitlements, countries should consider what incentives are necessary to recruit teachers in sufficient numbers.

WHO?

Teachers, both experienced and recent graduates, will require different preparation programmes to engage with migrants and to use various media effectively. Public authorities charged with integration management should, in co-ordination with educational institutions and ministries and/or teaching organisations, develop course standards and certification processes to ensure teachers enter the classroom with the tools they need. The authorities conducting these programmes, which in some cases may be language centres themselves, should also be involved.

HOW?

The dynamic between the teacher and migrant learner can greatly influence the chance for a successful outcome. To ensure that language teachers are placed in the best position to support migrant learners, countries should consider how to:

- Strengthen awareness of the specific needs and challenges of migrants through teacher preparation courses
- Adequately prepare teachers to engage with new ICT tools and teaching techniques
- Ensure that qualifications systems are tailored to meet course needs
- Create incentives to attract and retain teachers

Language teachers must be prepared to deal with specific cultural and linguistic issues of migrant classrooms in order to build up the language learning skills of their students. This requires a flexible and interactive approach. They must be trained to facilitate learning without relying on a common linguistic background in the student group. For teachers who will be leading specific courses on working life, it is essential they receive information on the realities that many migrants will face in the workplace (Pöyhönen and Tarnanen, 2015). Many teachers, even those who are otherwise highly trained, have received no training in responding to interculturalism[21] or plurilingualism. Recognising these gaps, several OECD countries have recently introduced or strengthened intercultural training as part of their teacher preparation programmes (see Box 11.1). It is important that pressure to reduce costs not result in inadequate time spent on teacher preparation, especially where teacher preparation is decentralised at the language centre level.

As stated, teaching adult migrants increasingly requires an understanding of new ways of teaching language through ICT. To harness the significant benefits of technology, such as universal access and increased differentiation, countries need to invest in specific teacher preparation. Teachers may have to use online tools, and in order to trust them as a reliable supplement to in-person lessons, they must have relevant digital competence. In ICT-integrated classrooms, teachers play both the role of teacher and also of facilitator in the learning process, encouraging self-direction in use of ICT tools. When teachers who are used to being in front of a class transition to distance or online learning, they will require support. Countries such as Germany and Sweden have recognised the need to train teachers to navigate digital literacy issues and apply new pedagogies, and, thus, have explicitly incorporated training on the use of ICT tools into the teacher certification process (see Box 11.2). The creation of open resource banks from which all teachers may draw, like in Germany and Austria, can enhance teaching. Such resources may also reduce teacher workloads, which may motivate teachers to make use of these tools in the classroom and outside of class.

Integration agencies should bring second-language specialists on to evaluate effectiveness of classroom methods and ensure teachers have been exposed to innovative techniques. In 2016, to improve the pedagogical orientation of its sfi (Swedish for Immigrants) programme, Sweden transitioned courses into the Municipal Adult Education System and called upon the National Agency for Education to create a syllabus and national models. More targeted interventions are also possible. Denmark has taken the approach of professionalising teachers of Danish as a second language, requiring completion of a 60 ECTS[22] programme "Education for Teachers of Danish as a Second Language for Adults" that contains modules on intercultural communication, language description theories, second language acquisition, and second language pedagogy. A Master in Danish as a Second Language is also offered at Copenhagen University. Educational institutions are uniquely positioned to inform course designers which approaches lead to durable language acquisition in the shortest time. For example, certain groups of low-literacy students may achieve greater outcomes with continuous feedback loops (Abrams and Gerber, 2013) or through introduction of participatory didactic methods that are less instruction-centred (Freire, 1994). Policies that can make use of this knowledge include investment in teacher training on provision of in-class opportunities for self-reflection and assessment as well as the creation of game-like courses on digital platforms. Germany is exploring methods for providing continuous feedback in its digital offerings through a "Learning Management System" (LMS) (see Box 10.1, Lesson 10). Courses designed to bring together groups with similar backgrounds and interests, such as specific, interactive courses for women, also provide comfortable spaces for the use of the participatory method (Nieuwboer and van't Rood, 2016). For instance, Belgium's language policy, approved in July 2018, acknowledges that language learning requires an active role for the learner, a safe learning environment, and a meaningful context.

Box 11.1. Preparation for Host Language Teachers within an Intercultural Context

Sweden provides SEK 100 million (EUR 9.3 million) per year for the education of teachers who will teach Swedish to immigrants, allowing teachers to receive 80% of their salary during leave of absence for studies related to Swedish as a second language (OECD, 2019).

To receive teacher certification in Switzerland within the Swiss "fide" framework, language teachers in the field of integration must demonstrate defined social competencies. Fide certified teachers in Switzerland should be qualified to offer assessment and guidance to migrants on their specific goals as well as to adapt courses to the specific needs of migrants in Switzerland (such as focusing on language usage in everyday life, teaching Swiss norms, and considering linguistic peculiarities of the Swiss national languages). These skills are described within a framework developed under the direction of the Swiss Federation for Adult Learning (SVEB). Since 2015, the fide Secretariat has issued more than 1 000 certificates in German, French and Italian. In the year 2018, more than 250 course trainers received this award.

Other countries have made recent strides to improve teacher preparation. Poland has provided intercultural training for language teachers since 2018. Since 2000, in the White Paper on Adult Education, interculturalism has been noted as one of the three pillars for the Irish adult education policy and practice, and in its Migrant Integration Strategy (2017-20), Ireland acknowledged the need for training for teachers on managing diversity.

Recruiting qualified teachers remains a challenge, as there is still significant scarcity. Low teacher salaries, coupled with strict certification requirements, may turn potential teachers toward traditional classrooms or the private sector. In some regions, there is a general shortage of teachers at all levels. Some countries have attempted to tackle the difficulty of employing teachers in regional and remote areas by broadening the qualifications to become a teacher (in the case of Australia's AMEP programme) or by engaging translators or interpreters to fill these gaps (in Belgium, a pilot programme was launched in 2018). Another option is to make use of "study centres," where professional staff can support self-study, to supplement courses, reducing the need for additional teacher hours. Where this occurs, it is important to ensure that these new educators meet certain standards of quality. This can be done through providing them with specific training on teaching language to migrants or by pairing them for a student-teaching period with an experienced educator (Ramboll, 2017). Academic partners should be engaged to ensure that certification standards have not been excessively relaxed. For instance, the AMEP Quality Assurance provider delivers regular professional development workshops to trainers and assessors.

Box 11.2. New tools, new trainings

Germany has developed digital tools that can be easily incorporated into the classroom or used for homework outside of class. However, having observed that teachers of the courses were often reluctant to use digital tools, Germany plans to mandate 16 training hours for teacher training on online tools. It will also ask teachers to introduce the tools in the first 100 "learning hours" of the migrant's language modules. The vhs-Lernportal, funded by the German Federal Ministry of Education and Research (BMBF) and implemented by the German Adult Education Association (DVV), also focuses on the development of teacher handouts and support materials. Based upon the high demand for these courses and materials, Germany perceives a long-unmet need for training in this area. Since implementation of the new, virtual, cost-free training programme in 2020, 2 400 courses have already been formed.

The Directorate of Reception, Support for Foreigners, and Nationality of the French Ministry of Interior, which has been charged with teacher support, also responded to the increased demand for distance learning caused by COVID-19 by recognising the need to incorporate feedback received on its digital offerings into future training of its language teachers. Switzerland also adapted teacher support measures in response to the pandemic, implementing webinars to present online tools and pedagogical methods and quickly upgrade the technical knowledge of teachers to best support learners (https://alice.ch/fr/themes/competences-de-base/promotion-innovante/competences-des-formateurs/serie-de-webinaires/).

The United Kingdom launched online resources to support English language teachers working with refugees who arrive with very low levels of English language in 2018. In addition, a toolkit was created in 2019, designed in co-operation with refugee and English language stakeholders, to be made available for English language teachers working with refugees.

Countries should also consider ways to make job opportunities as language teachers more attractive, through increased salary or benefits, in recognition of their professionalism. In the past, Sweden has introduced financial incentives for taking up preparation courses for teaching language to migrants (see Box 11.1). Germany increased the salary for freelance teachers from EUR 23 to EUR 35 per hour in July 2016 (OECD, 2017b), and again from EUR 35 to EUR 41 per hour in January 2021. Still, in many countries, host-language teaching jobs are characterised by part-time and temporary contracts, non-standard working hours, and lack of prestige (Kluzer, et al., 2011). Teachers, like migrants themselves, may need greater flexibility to choose when they teach and how many hours. Open resource banks, as discussed above, can relieve some pressure by reducing teacher workload outside the classroom. Continuing professional development that encourages an interpretive and reflective stance on teaching can reduce burnout, increase the teacher's sense of value, and at the same time increase course quality and outcomes.

12. Evaluate the impact of language training and act on the results

WHAT and WHY?

To date, language programmes across the OECD are rarely scientifically evaluated. This finding is somewhat surprising given that state-funded language training represents the bulk of public integration expenditures. In light of such major investments, countries should have a vital interest to ensure that their methods, training, and assessment services are relevant and effective in delivering the intended outcomes and that they are continuously updated and improved. The quality of the programme is especially important where participation is obligatory, or where countries have decided to impose penalties for failure to reach a certain language threshold. If migrants are to spend this time away from the labour market, they should do so in a way that will be most beneficial to them in the long run. Rigorously evaluating the impact of language training on labour market integration is also a necessary step to identify gaps and improve the effectiveness of available training options. The understanding of not only outcomes, but also of the "why" and "how" programmes are most effective, enables authorities to make tailored improvements that could deliver significant return on investment as the economic contributions of impacted migrants increases. It can provide valuable lessons regarding what measures could increase attendance by certain hard-to-reach groups, such as women and the elderly, as well as how to decrease drop-outs.

WHO?

Evaluating the impact of language training on language acquisition and on the labour market integration of participants should guide authorities in charge of organising and funding language programmes to make informed choices when choosing a course-provider, the overall methodology and incentives for both beneficiaries and course providers. A demonstrated impact on labour market integration is also a major driver of immigrants' motivation to participate in language training in the first place (see Lesson 2). In the wider sense, systematic evaluations of language training can be understood to constitute a duty towards taxpayers, wherever language schemes are financed from the public purse. Evaluation is a necessary condition for effective results-based management and can help authorities avoid overlap and waste.

HOW?

Evaluation enables countries to understand both whether migrants are learning the host-country language and whether higher language proficiency is actually facilitating access to the labour market. Ideally, language programmes incorporate a systematic and in-build element of evaluation from the very start. This allows the programme designers to test the validity of assumptions along the programme chain. To do this, the actor responsible for financing the programme must engage independent, external survey design experts who are asking the right questions. All relevant stakeholders, from financing (national or local authorities), to implementation (language schools), to consumer (migrants) should be included in the process.

To conduct an effective evaluation, a mechanism for baseline assessment is necessary. Information about the knowledge profile and any selection bias (i.e. motivation to choose vocational courses to rapidly enter employment) of learners can be collected before the beginning of the language course through a pre-assessment. Such an assessment should be based on consistent standards that ensure migrants are placed in an appropriate level. Ideally, it will also evaluate learning capacity, using, for example, educational background or tests of structural perception and logical thinking (i.e. Finland's Testipiste; Tammelin-Laine, et al. [2018]). Then, throughout the project evaluation, several check-in periods allow for measurement of medium-term effects. Analysing progress along the results chain allows the evaluator to understand what factors and institutional frameworks (e.g. course size, course duration, child care availability, use of virtual classrooms) increase success and to what extent, for which sub-groups.

To measure the effect of language training, it is important to recognise that migrants – especially new arrivals – will also enhance their proficiency in the host-country language in the absence of formal training. At the same time, especially where courses are lengthy, there is also a cost for migrants involved, as the time spent on language training is not available for job-search. Measuring the impact of language training thus requires an adequate comparison group that did not participate in the training. This, however, is often difficult, especially in cases where participation is expected to be near-universal for certain groups. Self-selection of language training participants is also an issue that a proper evaluation needs to address.

It is also essential to develop the right benchmarks based on the project goals. Language level targets (measured by successful exam results) are a convenient benchmark for evaluation of courses, but they may tell us little about effectiveness of the programme from a labour-market integration standpoint. Evaluators should question how the success for a language course can be measured beyond examination results, in particular taking into account labour market conditions and the vocational orientation of courses, as well as the profile of the students. Progress of the learner may be more important than outright achievement. Determining whether course participants are learning may require multiple methods, including satisfaction surveys, self-assessments, completion certificates, and portfolios. Evaluating the quality of courses could also involve monitoring service-provider performance and accreditation.

If improved labour-market performance is the goal, important questions also include whether migrants are likely to become self-sustaining enough to leave social or unemployment benefits or likely to take up a more highly qualified job, including in the longer term. In this context, it is interesting to assess whether vocational courses provide a greater chance of success in comparison to general language courses with the same target level. If it is feasible, checking in with migrants after the completion of the course to obtain information about labour market outcomes would better enable longer-term assessments of the viability of the programme, for example regarding whether participants are not only able to find, but to sustain, employment.

Embedding of evaluation design into language programmes has been rare in OECD countries to date. A proper impact evaluation is expensive and requires that part of the budget is reserved for that purpose. Data constraints are often a further obstacle, particularly given privacy law issues in some countries, which may prohibit the collection of biographical information that may impact learning outcomes. Insufficient participant numbers in smaller-scale programmes also pose a challenge. Rigorous evaluations require the selection of an adequate control-group to compare outcomes (usually attendance rates and test scores) before, during, and after the programme. Limited evaluation periods and the short duration of individual course types make it difficult to evaluate long-term successes. Wherever it is not possible to identify an adequate counterfactual group prior to programme implementation, comparing the outcomes of different cohorts of migrants is an alternative, which is often used to assess the impact of introduction programmes (Liebig and Huddleston, 2014). Good evaluations are almost invariably mixed method evaluations that use qualitative information to provide context in both design and interpretation.

Canada, Australia, France, Germany, and the United Kingdom are among the OECD countries, which have undertaken robust scientific evaluations of their language programmes. Canada, for instance, regularly requires evaluations to examine programme relevance, management, and impact of its Settlement Program (e.g. Immigration, Refugees and Citizenship Canada, Evaluation Division, 2017). Australia (AMEP Longitudinal Survey, see Yates, et al., 2015), France (ELIPA, see Bouvier, 2013) and Germany (Integration Panel, see Schuller, et al., 2011; Evaluation of the Integration Courses, see Tissot, et al., 2019) have launched longitudinal panels, in some cases comparing participants and non-participants. The United Kingdom's 'Equality Impact Assessment' has been used to evaluate the access to ESOL courses and their impact of changes for men and women and for different age, ethnic, and vulnerable groups (Department of Business, Innovation, and Skills, 2011). Still, particular attention should be paid to testing the design and organisation of the programmes in addition to its value added. To this end, the Nordic countries have taken the approach of testing the efficiency of new integration policy instruments via pilots prior to implementation. The Swedish bonus system for successful language course participants, for example, was piloted in the framework of a randomised experiment and discontinued after results indicated that the programme was only effective in metropolitan areas (Aslund and Engdahl, 2012).

Rigorous evaluation may have profound implications for policy makers in determining how much language training is necessary, how much flexibility to introduce, and how to identify and improve government-sanctioned course offerings. For example, a recent evaluation carried out for the Estonian Government identified significant unmet demand for language training and made specific recommendations regarding funding to improve the ability to hire enough quality teachers to meet that demand (Centar, 2018). Evaluators made the case for increasing flexible options by evaluating unemployment insurance fund data and tax data to examine two optional tracks offered by the Estonian Government against a control group of those who chose not to take a course, using a matching method. They found that a shorter "training card" course purchased on the market had a shorter lock-in effect and smaller dropout rate (13% v. 25%) than longer courses offered by the Unemployment Insurance Fund. Migrants who took a course had better results finding employment than those who did not, regardless of which course, though the positions were not necessarily higher paying (Kivi, et al., 2020).

An additional benefit of evaluation is knowing which programmes do not work before significant investment is made. In 2017, Canada's IRCC launched a Service Delivery Improvement initiative, investing nearly CAD 150M over five years and over CAD 35M on an ongoing basis to test innovative projects for improved effectiveness, subject to evidence-based monitoring over a lifecycle of 1-3 years.[23] The goal was not only to determine what works, but also what does not work and why. In some cases, insights gained through evaluation have led to programming being discontinued. For example, in Denmark, a decision to reduce welfare benefits in tandem with offering expanded and improved early language classes to refugees was discarded when it showed the reduction in benefits had no positive labour market effects. The study did find that increased course hours and quality improvements, notably through a focus on teacher training, yielded long-term benefits in spite of a significant lock-in effect (Arendt, et al., 2020).[24]

References

Abrams, S. and Gerber, H. (2013), "Achieving through the Feedback Loop: Videogames, Authentic Assessment, and Meaningful Learning," The English Journal, Vol. 103(1), pp. 95-103.

Ankestyrelsen (2020), Fravær fra danskuddannelse for flygtninge og familiesammenførte, National Board of Appeal of Denmark, Copenhagen, Denmark.

Arendt, J.N. et al. (2020), "Integrating Refugees: Language Training or Work-First Incentives?" NBER Working Paper No. 26834, National Bureau of Economic Research, Cambridge, MA, the United States.

Aslund, O. and Engdahl, M. (2012), "The Value of Earning for Learning: Performance bonuses in immigrant language training," IZA Discussion Paper No. 7118, IZA, Bonn, Germany.

Beacco, J.C. et al. (2014), "Linguistic integration of adult migrants: Guide to policy development and implementation," Council of Europe, Strasbourg, France.

Bouvier, G. (2013), "L'impact des cours de français pour les nouveaux migrants," Infos migrations, n. 55, Ministry of the Interior, Paris, France.

Chenven, L. (2004), "Getting to Work: A Report on How Workers with Limited English Skills Can Prepare for Good Jobs," AFL-CIO Working for America Institute, Washington, the United States.

Chiswick, B. and P. Miller (2014), "International Migration and the Economics of Language," IZA Discussion Paper No. 7880, IZA, Bonn, Germany.

Clausen, J. et al. (2009), "The Effect of Integration Policies on the Time until Regular Employment of Newly Arrived Immigrants: Evidence from Denmark," Labour Economics, Vol. 16, pp. 409-417.

Codagnone, C. and Kluzer, S. (2011), "ICT for the social and economic integration of migrants into Europe," JRC Scientific and Technical Report, EUR 24 719 EN, Seville, Spain.

Cooke, M. and Simpson, J., (2008) ESOL: A Critical Guide, Oxford University Press.

Damas de Matos, A. and T. Liebig (2014), "The qualifications of immigrants and their value in the labour market: A comparison of Europe and the United States", in OECD and European Union, Matching Economic Migration with Labour Market Needs, OECD Publishing, Paris. DOI: http://dx.doi.org/10.1787/9789264216501-9-en

Delander, L. et al. (2005), "Integration of Immigrants: The Role of language proficiency and experience", Evaluation Review, Vol. 29, No. 1, pp. 24-41.

Department for Justice and Equality (2016), "The Migrant Integration Strategy: A Blueprint for the Future," Government of Ireland, Dublin, Ireland.

Department for Business, Innovation, and Skills (2011), "English for Speakers of Other Languages (ESOL): Equality impact assessment," UK Government, London, UK.

Estonian Centre for Applied Research (CENTAR) and Tallinn University (2018), Estonian Language Training for Adults with Other Native Languages as Part of Estonian Integration and Employment Policy: Quality, Impact and Organisation, Tallinn, Estonia.

European Commission (2016), Mapping of good practices relating to social inclusion of migrants through sport: Final report to the DG Education and Culture of the European Commission, Brussels.

Fafo (2020), "'We have kept the wheels in motion.' The municipalities' integration work with refugees during the outbreak of the coronavirus," Fafo-rapport 2020:16.

Federal Ministry for Europe, Integration, and Foreign Affairs (2016), Integration Report, Expert Council on Integration, Vienna, Austria, https://www.bmeia.gv.at/fileadmin/user_upload/Zentrale/Integration/Integrationsbericht_2016/Integration_Report_2016_EN_WEB.pdf.

Freire, P. (1994), Pedagogy of hope: reliving pedagogy of the oppressed, Continuum, New York.

Friedenberg, J. et al. (2014), Effective Practices in Workplace Language Training, TESOL Publications, Alexandra, the United States.

Galvão, I. and S. Cabrita (2020), Notebook of Theatrical Practices for the Learning of the Language, Conselho Português para os Refugiados, Lisbon, Portugal.

Gortz, M., Heinesen, E., Husted, L. and Hald, S. (2006), "Benchmarking Analysis of Danish Municipalities' Integration Policies in the period 1999-2005," Institute for Local Government Studies, Copenhagen, Denmark.

Hartikainen, A., Ahola, M., Apiola, M. and Sutinen, E. (2020), "The immigrant integration online training programme in Finland." (forthcoming).

Hennessy, S., Harrison, D. and Wamakote, L, (2010), "Teacher factors influencing classroom use of ICT in Sub-Saharan Africa," Itupale online journal of African studies, Vol. 2(1), pp. 39-54.

Immigration, Refugees and Citizenship Canada, Evaluation Division (2017), Evaluation of Settlement Program, Government of Canada, Ottawa, Canada.

Isphording, I. (2013), "Disadvantages of Linguistic Origin: Evidence from Immigrant Literacy Scores", Ruhr Economic Papers No. 397, Bochum/Dortmund/Duisburg/Essen, Germany.

Kivi, L., Somer, M. and Kallaste, E. (2020), "Language Training for Unemployed Non-natives: Who Benefits the Most?" Baltic Journal of Economics, Vol. 20, No. 1, pp. 34-58.

Kluzer, S., Ferrari, A. and Centeno, C. (2011), "Language Learning by Adult Migrants: Policy challenges and ICT responses," Joint Research Centre Institute for Prospective Technological Studies, Seville, Spain.

Korte, W.B, and Husing, T. (2007), Benchmarking access and use of ICT in European schools 2006: Results from Head Teacher and A Classroom Teacher Surveys in 27 European countries. e-L earning Papers, 2(1), 1-6.

Kozar, O. and Yates, L. (2019), "Factors in Language Learning after 40: Insights from a Longitudinal Study," International Review of Applied Linguistics in Language Teaching, 57(2), 181-204.

Krumm, H. J., and Plutzar, V. (2008), Tailoring language provision and requirements to the needs and capacities of adult migrants, Retrieved from LIAM. https://rm.coe.int/CoERMPublicCommonSearchServices/DisplayDCTMContent.

Liebig, T. and Huddleston, T. (2014), "Labour market integration of immigrants and their children: Developing, activating and using skills", in OECD, International Migration Outlook 2014, OECD Publishing, Paris. DOI: http://dx.doi.org/10.1787/migr_outlook-2014-5-en.

Liebig, T and Tronstad, T. (2018). "Triple disadvantage? A first overview of the integration of refugee women," OECD Social, Employment, and Migration Working Papers, (216), pp. 1-37.

Lochmann, A., Rapoport, H., Speciale, B. (2019), "The Effect of Language Training on Immigrants' Economic Integration Empirical Evidence from France," European Economic Review, Vol. 113(C), pp. 265-296.

Loewen, S., Isbell, D., Sporn, Z. (2020), "The Effectiveness of App-based Language Instruction for Developing Receptive Linguistic Knowledge and Oral Communicative Ability," Foreign Language Annals, Vol. 53, pp. 209-233.

Mayer, R. E. (2019), "Thirty years of research on online learning." Applied Cognitive Psychology, Vol.

33(2), pp. 152-159.

Ministry of Aliyah and Integration (2019), Guide to Ulpan Study, Tenth Ed.

New Zealand Government (2019), New Zealand Migrant Settlement and Integration Strategy: Outcomes Indicators 2018, Supplementary Report, New Zealand Immigration.

Nieuwboer, C., and van't Rood, R. (2016), "Learning language that matters: A pedagogical method to support migrant mothers without formal education experience in their social integration in Western countries," International Journal of Intercultural Relations, Vol. 51, 29-40.

OECD (2007), Jobs for Immigrants (Vol. 1): Labour Market Integration in Australia, Denmark, Germany and Sweden, OECD Publishing, Paris, http://dx.doi.org/10.1787/9789264033603-en.

OECD (2014), Jobs for Immigrants (Vol. 4): Labour Market Integration in Italy, OECD Publishing, Paris, https://doi.org/10.1787/9789264214712-en.

OECD (2016), OECD Review of Policies to Improve the Effectiveness of Resource use in Schools, School Resources Review, Country Background Report: Sweden, http://www.oecd.org/education/school/CBR_OECD_SRR_SE-FINAL.pdf.

OECD (2017a), Making Integration Work: Family Migrants, Making Integration Work, OECD Publishing, Paris, https://doi.org/10.1787/9789264279520-en.

OECD (2017b), Finding their Way: Labour Market Integration of Refugees in Germany," OECD Publishing, Paris, https://www.oecd.org/els/mig/Finding-their-Way-Germany.pdf.

OECD (2018), International Migration Outlook 2018, OECD Publishing, Paris, https://doi.org/10.1787/migr_outlook-2018-en.

OECD (2019), International Migration Outlook 2019, OECD Publishing, Paris, https://doi.org/10.1787/c3e35eec-en.

OECD/European Union (2018), Settling In 2018: Indicators of Immigrant Integration, OECD Publishing, Paris/European Union, Brussels, https://doi.org/10.1787/9789264307216-en.

Ofsted (2008), "ESOL in the post-compulsory learning and skills sector: an evaluation," Ofsted, London, the United Kingdom.

Pöyhönen, S., and Tarnanen, M. (2015), Integration policies and adult second language learning in Finland. Adult language education and migration: Challenging agendas in policy and practice, Routledge.

Ramboll (2007a), Evaluation of the Nationwide Integration Courses, Federal Ministry of the Interior, Berlin, Germany.

Ramboll (2007b), Med Moduler Som Motor: Evaluering af implementeringen af danskuddannelsesloven, Copenhagen, Denmark.

Ramboll (2017), Evaluering af danskuddannelsesreformen 2017, Copenhagen, Denmark.

Ramboll (2020), Evaluerig af puljen til virksomhedsorganiseret dansundervisning, Copenhagen, Denmark.

Rideout, V., and Katz, V. S. (2016). Opportunity for All? Technology and Learning in Lower-Income Families, In Joan Ganz Cooney Center at Sesame Workshop. Joan Ganz Cooney Center at Sesame Workshop, New York, NY.

Roberts, C. (2003), "English to Speakers of Other Languages (ESOL) in the workplace: review of research and related literature", NRDC, London, the United Kingdom.

Rossner, R. (2014a), "Providers of courses for adult migrants: Self-assessment handbook," Council of Europe, Strasbourg, France.

Rossner, R. (2014b), "Quality Assurance in the provision of language education and training for adult migrants: Guidelines and options," Council of Europe, Strasbourg, France.

Sarvimäki, M. and Hämäläinen, K. (2012), "Assimilating Immigrants: the Impact of an integration programme", Discussion Paper 306, Helsinki Center of Economic Research, Helsinki, Finland.

Sarvimäki, M. and Hämäläinen, K. (2016), "Integrating Immigrants: The Impact of Restructuring Active Labor Market Programmes," Journal of Labor Economics, Vol 34, Issue 2, pp 479-508.

Schuller, K. et al. (2011), "Integration Panel: Results of a longitudinal study on the effectiveness and sustainability of integration courses," Federal Office for Migration and Refugees, Nürnberg, Germany.

Shadiev, R., Hwang, W. Y., and Liu, T. Y. (2018), "Investigating the effectiveness of a learning activity supported by a mobile multimedia learning system to enhance autonomous EFL learning in authentic contexts," Educational Technology Research and Development, 66(4), 893-912.

Significant (2010), Evaluatierapport Inburgering in Nederland, The Hague, The Netherlands.

Social Compass (2019), Evaluation of the Adult Migration English Program New Business Model, Commissioned by Department of Education and Training for the Department of Home Affairs, Australia.

Špačková, L. and Štefková, J. eds. (2006), "Libraries as Gateways to the Integration of Immigrants in the EU," Multicultural Center Prague, Prague, Czech Republic. Asgary, R. and N. Seger (2011), "Barriers to Health Care Access among Refugee Asylum Seekers", Journal of Health Care for the Poor and Underserved, Vol. 22, No. 2, pp. 506 522, May.

Tammelin-Laine, T., et al. (2018), "Predicting Placement Accuracy and Language Outcomes in Immigrants' L2 Finnish Education," in Davis, J.M., et al. (eds.), Useful Assessment and Evaluation in Language Education (p.149-165), Washington: Georgetown University Press.

Tissot, A., et al. (2019), Zwischenbericht I zum Forschungsproject "Evaluation der Integrationskurse (EvIk)," Zentrale Ergebnisse, Nürnberg, Germany.

Tomlinson, C. A., and Imbeau, M. B. (2010), Leading and Managing a Differentiated Classroom, Alexandria, VA: ASCD.

UNESCO (2004), Study of best practices in education based on ICT: Mexico, UNESCO, Mexico City.

Wienberg, J., Dutz, G., and Grotlüschen, A. (2019, accepted), "Language Learning of Migrants: Empirical evidence from the German integration course system," Germany.

Yates, L., et al. (2015), Adult Migrant English Program (AMEP) longitudinal study 2011-14: Final report, Sydney, Australia.

Zorlu, A. and Hartog, J. (2018), "The Impact of Language on Socioeconomic Integration of Immigrants," IZA Discussion Paper No. 11485, IZA, Bonn, Germany.

Notes

[1] A recent study of the impact of Dutch-language learning in the Netherlands indicates that, controlling for endogenous factors, not only does Dutch proficiency increase the likelihood for migrants to enter employment by 30 percentage points, but it also increases their feeling of social integration even more, by 50 percentage points (Zorlu and Hartog, 2018).

[2] The term "humanitarian migrant" typically refers to persons who have successfully applied for asylum and have been granted some sort of protection or have been resettled through humanitarian programmes outside the asylum procedure. For the sake of simplicity, this booklet considers all recipients of protection – be it refugee status, subsidiary or temporary protection – to be humanitarian migrants, given that the groups benefit from similar (and often identical) language integration measures.

[3] Countries have taken a variety of strategic actions based on differing philosophies of integration (language and civics training versus work-first incentives, for example). Countries like the United States have historically preferred work-first incentives, leaving language training to local governments or the not-for-profit sector. Others, such as France (in 2007) and Germany (in 2005), have chosen to implement language courses alongside civics instruction. These positions reflect cultural differences, as well as differences in the makeup of each nation's economy, and there is no one-size-fits-all policy response. For many OECD countries, however, there has been a gradual shift to a blended approach, combining language with work-first integration (Arendt et al., 2020).

[4] A 2009 pilot voucher programme by Citizenship and Immigration Canada significantly increased enrolment by informing randomly selected newcomers about available free language training. The news release reporting the result of the Language Training Vouchers pilot project is available here: https://www.canada.ca/en/news/archive/2010/11/vouchers-work-more immigrants-enrolling-language classes.html.

[5] A tax-free "Danish language bonus" of DKK 6 242 (in 2019) is available to refugees and family reunited with refugees who do not receive social benefits and have passed a Danish language course level 2 or higher. Municipalities receive subsidies when a refugee or family member obtains employment, starts education, or passes a final test in Danish. For each eligible migrant to pass a final test in the Danish language, the municipality receives a subsidy of DKK 33 959 (in 2019).

[6] The Immigrant Citizens Survey asked immigrants to assess their needs for integration and evaluated how effective policies were in meeting these needs. A pilot took place over 2011 and 2012 in Belgium, France, Germany, Hungary, Italy, Portugal, and Spain. See http://www.immigrantsurvey.org/about.html.

[7] Language acquisition is critical for refugee women in particular. Research shows that refugee women who become proficient in their host country's language are 40 percentage points more likely to be employed (Liebig and Tronstad, 2018).

[8] Integration agencies in several countries have noted that women may not be able to participate in regular courses for "family or cultural reasons," but they may be more likely to access programming if classes are homogenous or if they are clearly informed of their rights along with their husbands (OECD, 2017b). For more information, see Monica Li (2018), "Integration of Migrant Women," European Commission, https://ec.europa.eu/migrant-integration/feature/integration-of-migrant-women or Nino Simic et al. (2018), "New in the Nordic Countries: Labour Market Inclusion of Migrants," Nordic Council of Ministers, https://issuu.com/nordicwelfare/docs/new-in-the-nordic-countries-en-web. Moreover, research into academic performance of women and girls suggests that outcomes and attitudes may be slightly improved in gender-homogenous learning environments (Dustmann, Ku, and Kwak, 2017; Riggers-Piehl, Lim and King, 2018).

[9] During a six-month study in Helsinki, Testipiste observed that only 20 students moved to the slow track from the regular track after beginning a course. Both Testipiste and Finnish public employment service offices have also made use of databases to share information with educational institutions and teachers. Teachers are able to access information about placement tests, as well as labour market programmes and educational courses undertaken. They have been educated to interpret test results to modify their teaching to support specific needs.

[10] The municipality of Wroclaw introduced a volunteer-based "Tongues of the World" programme in recognition of the financial barrier many migrants encountered to accessing language courses. The programme also encourages intercultural communication and community acceptance. See https://www.wnjs.pl/en/about-the-project/.

[11] Presentation of the 104: http://www.104.fr/presentation.html.

[12] Switchboard is funded by the U.S. Office of Refugee Resettlement (ORR) and implemented by the IRC. The IRC has also partnered with the Lutheran Immigrant Refugee Service (LIRS) to provide employment-related trainings and technical assistance. For more information, see https://switchboardta.org.

[13] Various studies have concluded that language is a means to transmit culture. Language is shaped by culture because it is the primary means of communication within a culture. Thus, it is recognised that cultural proficiency can enhance language learning and vice versa. Lafayette, R. C. (1988). *Integrating the teaching of culture into the foreign language classroom* (in A. J. Singerman (Ed.), Toward a new integration of language and culture (pp. 47-62). Middlebury, VT: Northeast Conference); Nguyen, T. T. T. (2017). Integrating culture into language teaching and learning: Learner outcomes. *The Reading Matrix: An International Online Journal*, 17(1), 145-155.

[14] Studies have also pointed to the advantage of collaborative versus individual learning in the context of second-language acquisition (Shadiev, Hwang and Liu, 2018). Mobile tools can provide opportunities for autonomous study, but they will likely be more effective if they also enable information sharing and feedback from fellow learners and/or a teacher. For more, see also Wu, R. (2019). "The Effectiveness of MALT on Vocational College English Teaching," *Journal of Language Teaching and Research*, 10(3), 641-647.

[15] For the German example offered on Deutsche Welle, see http://www.dw.com/de/deutsch-lernen/s-2055.

[16] For analysis of policies to support ICT inclusion for disadvantaged groups, see the OECD's Digital Economy Outlook 2017, https://doi.org/10.1787/9789264276284-en.

[17] For examples, see www.taalklas.nl; www.alfabetiseren.nl.

[18] For more information, see https://slovake.eu/en.

[19] Arffman, a provider of immigrant integration training and specialist in distance learning in Finland, started an online course for residents of Lapland in 2015. The company reported a drop-out rate of only 3% in 2019. Among students that studied a minimum of 200 days, 52% reached the target language level of B1.1 or above (see Hartikainen, et al., 2020).

[20] Lack of technical support in the classroom is a significant barrier to ICT integration from the teacher's perspective (Korte and Husing, 2007). Even in highly supported and resourced schools, teachers have demonstrated that, without proper preparation, "technophobia" will be a major barrier to uptake of new technologies. (UNESCO, 2004). Teachers' age, attitudes, expertise, and lack of knowledge needed to evaluate the use of ICT in teaching are prominent factors hindering teacher preparedness (Hennessy et al., 2010).

[21] Interculturalism is defined as "the need to frame policy and practice in the context of serving a diverse population." In the case of education policy, this requires the development of curricula, materials, modes of assessment, and delivery methods which take diversity as the norm.

[22] The European Credit Transfer and Accumulation System (ECTS) is used by the European Higher Education Area as a standard means for comparing academic credits based on volume of learning. 60 ECTS credits is the equivalent of a full year of study.

[23] Over 100 projects have been funded under Canada's Service Delivery Improvement Initiative to date, and a second intake process was launched in fall 2020 with a focus on supporting the adaptation and recovery of newcomers and the settlement service sector following the COVID-19 pandemic. Funded projects under this second intake will begin in fall 2021.

[24] A recent French study used random assignment to language treatment around a testing threshold, finding that two years after completion of classes, 100 hours of language training increased labour force participation by 15 to 27 percentage points (Lochmann, et al., 2019). A similar study of the decision to develop individual integration plans in Finland found that migrants were subsequently offered more language hours and obtained significant improvement in employment outcomes (Sarvimäki and Hämäläinen, 2016).